'24-7' Multi-Cultural Workers Find Diversity Recipe to Heal a Troubled World

'24-7' Multi-Cultural Workers Find Diversity Recipe to Heal a Troubled World

Jackie Chase

www.adventuretravelpress.com

24-7: Multi-Cultural Workers Find Diversity Recipe to Heal a Troubled World
By Jackie Chase

www.adventuretravelpress.com, Lady Lake, FL 32159
Copyright © 2017 by Jackie Chase

24-7: Multi-Cultural Workers Find Diversity Recipe to Heal a Troubled World
By Jackie Chase
***Color Print: ISBN- 978-1-937630-30-0
E-book: ISBN- 978-1-937630-31-7
Grayscale Print: ISBN 978-1-937630-29-4
www.JackieChase.com; www.CulturesOfTheWorld.com

Publisher's Cataloging-In-Publication Data
(Prepared by The Donohue Group, Inc.)

Names: Chase, Jackie.
Title: '24-7' multi-cultural workers find diversity recipe to heal a
    troubled world / Jackie Chase.
Other Titles: '24 7' multi-cultural workers find diversity recipe to
    heal a troubled world | Twenty-four-seven multi-cultural workers
    find diversity recipe to heal a troubled world | Multi-cultural
    workers find diversity recipe to heal a troubled world
Description: [Lady Lake, Florida] : www.adventuretravelpress.com,
    [2017] | Includes resources for further reading.
Identifiers: ISBN 978-1-937630-31-7 (ebook) | ISBN 978-1-937630-30-0
    (color print) |ISBN 978-1-937630-29-4 (grayscale print)
Subjects: LCSH: Diversity in the workplace. | Corporate culture. |
    Cruise ships--Employees--Interviews. | Tourism--Employees--Inter-
    views. | Tourism--International cooperation. | LCGFT: Interviews.
Classification: LCC HF5549.5.M5 C43 2017 (print) | LCC HF5549.5.M5
    (ebook) | DDC 658.3008--dc23 3

Foreword

This book highlights several means and benefits of working effectively with a very diverse workforce. First, they embrace it as a means of delivering their service. Second, respect for others on many dimensions is critical and third, they continually train to achieve excellence. Thus, they reinforce the goals/values routinely. Many of the principles can apply to a range of organizations to enable them to achieve their mission/goals.

Dwain Celistan, *Managing Partner, Diversity Practice*
DHR International

'24-7'

Contents

Introduction: PART I: The Crew Speaks

Introduction: PART II: The Resort Floats

PART I
introduction: the crew speaks

"The sea, once it casts its spell, holds one in its net of wonder forever."
Jacques Cousteau

These stories flow from the mouths of a ship's crew, sharing with the interviewer a behind-the-scenes look at secrets that create the magic of cruising. They tell about the special lives of crew members and what it feels like to be on a team with folks from seventy-nine cultures. Hidden within each story, there are some gems, highlighted in purple text. These crew stories could impact our lives at work and play; they offer hope for a future world where we might discover the truth that each of us has a special role as we live together in a house called earth. The reader may, like crew members, celebrate, and learn from, our differences and contributions, while making a friend.

We may learn that even though we might have grown up in different cultures, we are still part of a large human family. We can polish the gems gleaned from these pages, learn about the other members of our world family, and respect them. The author, Jackie Chase, has traveled to over 100 of the world's cultures, often primitive ones, and has observed what all of us have in common. Her five major books have together garnered over 30 awards and stimulate our desire to understand our human similarities and differences. Today's cruise ships show how crew members (like these from 79 cultures) work together in a confined space for months at a time and act as a team.

The story of respect for our world's many cultures started centuries ago at the dawn of religion. Ethics rules developed as humankind wrestled with the similarities and differences they observed in contacts with other people. The family played a strong role in forming a protection for its members, and families grew into tribes, and tribes into villages, and villages into nations. The language-barrier hurdle, plus fear and the survival instinct, contributed to friction among groups. Sometimes, religious passions seem to hurt, rather than help, tolerance and friendship. Modern western nations have adopted various rules to outlaw discrimination based on a long list of human attributes and associations, such as gender, race, religion, and a much longer set of conditions.

Part I emphasizes the stories of how a variety of people, representing many of those attributes and childhood experiences, have come together by the hundreds to live and work together in a marine environment the width of a couple of city lots. These workers must rely on each other's sincere cooperation, and even friendship, to carry out the mission of the cruise line: to please the guests. Though these interviews tell the tale of just one such ship at one point in time, the stories can represent imitation opportunities at any hotel, resort, business, charity, or government agency.

In a world fraught with local, regional, and national conflicts, the small miracle of a well-managed cruise ship deserves a second look, for it seems that anything worthwhile requires thought, planning, execution, and maintenance of set standards. The people at Royal Caribbean International seem to have met the test. The author looked at this, not from a scientific or academic view, but rather as a reporter, sharing with readers some candid observations. Royal Caribbean International has challenged the earth's communities of employers, cities, and nations to take the lessons to heart and apply the "ten-foot-rule" [explained in the book] to daily lives.

The stories shared with the author detail a variety of backgrounds of the people who have found joy in the common mission of pleasing guests. Blended with great ships, delicious food, elegant staterooms, diverting activities, and breathtaking destinations, the addition of staff from all around the globe frosts the cake and fills a guest's memories with that unique and special cultural extra that brings them back for more cruising adventures while enriching their lives.

Part II emphasizes crew stories about the mission of Royal Caribbean International from the business and entertainment side of managing and running a resort on water. All workers associated with this cruise line or any other employer that encourages multi-cultural respect should feel great pride in being associated with such an organization. Each reader, guest, manager, or employee, as stories unfold, can absorb, and imitate the ideas and perhaps change a life or organization, possibly their own.

chapter 1: sailor number one

"To me, being at sea is an obsession."

Johnny Faevelen, Captain, Allure of the Seas, Norway

Captain Johnny

"Don't forget you promised to marry us on Tuesday in Haiti!"

The email came on Sunday afternoon minutes before Captain Johnny was about to embark on an eight-day Caribbean journey.

I sat down with Captain Johnny Faevelen of Norway and asked him about his life as a cruise-boat captain.

The captain responded to a question about the difficulty in dealing with the embedded customs and traits of such a diverse team, "No, it's not a problem, because you have to be at their level. As a manager, you need to speak their language, understanding them. That cultural training comes through, but my many years of cultural training, on the job has given me the experience to understand this diversity. There is a huge difference between a Norwegian and a Finn, even though we share the same borders. We differ on how we react to things, how we think, and how we are. As for being a manager, it's a matter of making them feel comfortable when talking to them. If you treat people with respect, you receive respect in return. Talking to people [while putting them at ease] helps them feel good about their decisions."

When asked, if he would rather work with a variety of cultures or all Norwegians, Captain Johnny Faevelen responded:

"This is wonderful, compared to working with one nationality. The advantage is that you have a different way of thinking, and you are not the stereotype. If you were a group of Norwegians, you would know how each would react, and the result might be that there is only one way to do something without question. That goes for all nationalities, whether American, Filipino, or Jamaican. To get all these ideas into a big bowl and then review how to do things is what makes Royal Caribbean International's product so unique."

Norway: Where the midnight sun never sets

The idea of marrying a couple on the island of Haiti, although a first for Captain Johnny, added spice to the typical day of needing to show up in three places at once. Overcoming a vast number of challenges defines a great captain.

Strangers, all twenty-two hundred employees from nearly eighty different countries, create a unique working environment. Over six thousand guests, from dozens of countries, realize that diversity enriches their cruising experience.

"My life is about missing," the captain says. "Being a sailor, you miss your family and friends, and having said that, I miss my friends [and ship family while home], but that's a traveler's and sailor's life. I would not say my job comes with pressure, but I have to be that certain type of person, and I miss that when I am out just being myself. And I can leave my stripes at the door when in executive meetings because they know I am the captain. It's not about authority but being together and accepting."

Showing off port and starboard socks

Effective communication with different cultures challenges the best of us. Rules about proper behavior affect verbal and non-verbal communication. Cul-

tures provide people with specific ways of thinking, seeing, hearing, and inter-
preting their worlds."

.

"Shine out. No matter where we are from, we are Allure of the Seas team!"

David Adams, Inventory Manager, Guyana

In 1983, exactly twenty years after Guyana officially said goodbye to slavery, David Adams joined **Royal Caribbean International**, realizing very quickly the similarities in the ways of living on a ship and in his home country.

Storage room on Deck

Guyana has cultural diversity, with all seven nationalities living, working, and playing as one. Mr. Adams came to the ship as a technical storekeeper, a petty officer position, a leadership role. He occupied a prime position to integrate his knowledge of diverse cultures and share his expertise with the people around him. He believes in no barriers between cultures. Everyone has the same ability to do whatever he/she wants to do, and Royal Caribbean International offers many opportunities for growth.

"I think one of the things I was very impressed with was the equal opportunity that was given to each and every person by Royal Caribbean International so you had the opportunity to grow. It's only you, yourself, who needs to put that initiative there," David states with a firm belief.

David: "Share what you know"

The inventory manager has responsibility for the total logistics of the ship, which includes buying everything needed to run the hotel operation onboard the ship. The marine side handles its own procurement. The inventory manager's tasks begin with the special chocolates found on guest's pillows at night and include linens, all the food and beverage consumables, and much of everything else that will make the guests' vacation like no other. Daily planning with teamwork enables and supports that success. The foundation of the operation lies in the motivation given to the crew members. The beginning of their day lays the foundation, with everything passing through them and disseminating to all others. Whatever happens on the ship, the procurement team is the root.

"Guest expectations as well as Royal Caribbean International's are high, so with each task, we need to make sure we go beyond those expectations. Get the team to realize that every customer is important. When a person leaves this ship, they leave with a smile," says David.

"Because in each country the cultures are so different, what might be good for you might not be good for me. A controlled cultural diversity class allows all team members to understand all ways of expression. Working on the same common goal of meeting the guests' expectations becomes easier with everyone understanding each other."

Plenty of eggs

David says, "I might to tell you something that is pleasant in a harsh way without any feelings because our stock [Guyana] is very strong, and we are aggressive speakers. But coming from an Oriental country, the crews are more timid, quieter, so my aggressiveness toward them may look intimidating. So, to really balance that out, the best thing to do is to hear about all the cultural experiences in order to understand, so that even if one hears a guy from St. Vincent use a word which we consider bad, it's not, because it's a part of his culture. So now, we have everybody understanding each other and all working for the same common goal: to meet the guests' expectations. People take a lot of things for granted, and they don't understand how it affects the other individual. If I touch your fist and it means a good job, it's not like I want to cuff you or hit you. It's just that I want to say you are doing a good job."

Buying into the same gestures, emotions, and slang helps integrate crew members, and before long, one hears the St. Vincent crew member saying to the Filipino, "How's it going?" in the Filipino's language. So, each uses each other's slang.

Integration is a positive force on the ship. Because the crew members spend so much time together, they become an extended family, a part of each other. Respect tells the whole story. When sharing a cabin with another, the first person a crew member sees when he wakes is his cabin mate. Helping that person creates a unique togetherness for an unbeatable operation.

Liquid eggs used in recipes

"Crew members are very protective of each other. They look out for each other and watch each other's backs." David remembers a situation where a crew member had problems with locals on an island, and their crew member friends came to help by representing them. "Yes, you have the situation where a person is an informant because of jealousy, but in general, they take care of each other. A crew member may associate with a guest on board. He may meet a guest outside the ship, take the guest to a special restaurant where locals go, not tourists, and introduce the guest to local food. In my vocational experience, that is a wow for a crew member to take that kind of personal touch with the guest," explains David.

David's better half works on board and often tells him stories of individuals coming aboard and telling her they could not believe she remembered their drink preference from when she served them on the *Oasis of the Seas*.

He says, "It is the culture of the ship. People think you are forced to do this, but it's not so. It's genuine love for what you do. You may come on board the ship, not as a waiter but to handle luggage or polish woodwork, and you get into service areas and you've developed into this person who genuinely cares. And you are becoming a better person. You come in one way, and you leave another. You may have been stubborn when you came [in]. You go back home a changed person. Your families say you never care, and now you care."

Face to face on "I-95"

David spent part of his bonus last year buying a small stereo for each of his team members. Now they can play their own music and practice for the karaoke, which has become a sort of competition among the group of nineteen. At least once a week, the group gets together to "vent," even if one can't sing. This creates a healthy way to reduce stress, resulting in a more productive and organized attitude. As David says, "You are not at home but you are still at home. You allow everything to be a part of you. The only way to make guests happy is to change and be receptive to change. I have to do everything within myself to come to work, smile, and create an environment that is workable, happy, so that our people are happy, and this transfers from you to the guest. I try to ensure that I provide an environment that is full of all the possible tools to get the job done."

Guyana: Only country in South America where English is the main language.

By creating a friendly and organized working space, team members become more productive when eliminating stress.

Team leaders concentrate on the positive. An exceptional job gets a pat on the back or "great job" in front of peers, building confidence. The negatives remain unspoken in public, reserved for private discussion with the idea of emphasizing the right thing, which resolves the issue. Finding what someone did wrong, and showing him the right way instead, boosts morale.

"I think the other thing we do well is always the right thing to the wrong. You physically go there and show them how to do it. So, they get an understanding of how to do it, and this is how it should be done, and we do this daily. Always allow them to come to you. About anything."

"I feel, as a manager, your presence in the workplace is a boost, as when your employee sees you around, they are confident. We have common respect from crew to manager. I think one of the things the senior managers do on the ship is ensuring the crew have their social life needs met onboard. We have done so many things to enhance that, like you are giving them a life to look forward to with parties. Like we say, it's a home away from home. I can say with conviction, there is no company in the world that can say the same, that we have done so much to ensure happiness for our 63,000 employees, whether ship board or shore side, since we started the company. We have great leaders in Adam Goldstein and Richard Fain. I think it is their conviction that the crew must be happy. The crew is the backbone of this organization. The crew is what makes it happen," says David.

chapter 3: fix that bug!

"I'm very conscious when I leave home. Anything can happen to me, or somebody I love, and at that moment, we are where we are. You have to make the most of every day."

Flo Belo, Information Technology, Argentina

College in the United States gave Flo Belo a taste of the world. Settling down back home in Argentina never occurred to her. Thoughts of world travel gave her the courage to apply for a cruise job. The bartending experience she gained while working for tuition met the requirements for applying to the cruise line as a bartender.

Her friends at sea are family

That first contract at sea means you begin to count Mondays. How else would you keep track of time?

Four friends from Argentina, also working on the cruise ship with Flo, became lifelines to home and customs until each received new assignments on other ships, a hard lesson about quick separation on such short notice. Flo developed new friendships that came with new challenges. This brought into focus Flo's discovery that life revolves around people as much as around the experiences that come with world travel.

Alarm clocks go off at the same time every day. Cruise employees have very few free days to sleep late. Long hours of duty call for learning discipline, sort of a mixture of Big Brother/Army. Flo remarked with a wide smile, "For sure I thought hiking down the Grand Canyon felt challenging. I came here and said to myself, "Take me back to the Grand Canyon. The time I spend away from home, I want to go back and join my family and friends, but I want to travel as well. Everybody should have one contract to experience the challenges Royal Caribbean International offers."

Pato: National sport of Argentina combines polo and basketball (played on horseback).

For Flo Belo, motivation comes from her team, which invests both energy and training in helping her reach her goals. Although the crew speaks English for cruise ship work, the accents of different nationalities make it difficult to understand her fellow crew at times. Eager to assist, team members play an active role in assisting others with language difficulties.

"I used to drink Red Bull," Flo admits, but now she lives the healthiest way she can, including taking a regimen of vitamins. The responsibilities of her position in IT (Information Technology) require she become involved with everything. The whole ship uses digital equipment for even the smallest of items, like when you go to the gym. And if the soda machine does not work, or your key card does not open your cabin door, Flo needs to be on top of that technology. Monitoring technical systems on the hotel side ensures everything runs properly. The strategies for a management job involve knowing how to make it all happen.

Homesickness means only one thing, missing mom's food. When as a child you eat another home-cooked meal, you say to yourself, "Oh no, not again," but you can almost taste those meals when away from home. It's also the little snippets of life that sift through our memory banks that bring us back to home, like for Flo, when sitting in her home kitchen, drinking *maté* with a friend. Suddenly you become aware of those memories.

Argentineans, born with the art of drinking *maté*, bond in friendship when sharing the same straw and the hollow gourd full of hot tea. *Yerba maté*, a widely cultivated evergreen tree, can grow up to sixty feet tall in the wild. Ancient sixteenth-century South American Indians discovered its power to relieve fatigue due to its exhilarating effects. Dried, chopped, and then ground, leaves of the *yerba maté* tree become a powdery mixture called *yerba*. The *bombilla*, or straw, traditionally made of silver, has a flared end full of tiny holes that, when submerged, acts as a filter to strain out the leafy fragments. The *cuia*, or gourd, holds the thick mass of leaves. One individual acts as the *cebador*, or the server, ensuring the tea reaches the proper temperature and tastes good. The first brew, called the *maté del zonzoor*, or *maté* of the fool, may fall short of acceptable. The server passes the drink around the circle of friends up to a dozen times, depending on the quality of the *yerba* used. The better-quality *yerba* lasts longer, producing a stronger brew. Sometimes those in the *ronda*, or circle, might warn the user by saying, "Bring the talking gourd." Teenagers might say in Argentina, *"No es un microfono,"* or, it's not a microphone, meaning the user is taking too much time with the gourd of *maté* as if using a microphone to deliver a speech. The tough, leathery leaves of the *yerba mate* tree, similar to those of a holly tree, produce the medicinal and refreshing beverage. *Maté* bars thrive in South America, like coffee cafes in Europe and North America. The art of drinking *maté* has deep cultural roots.

Spicy food, sharing *maté*, or watching the tango remind us of the passion of Argentinians. Just translating the lyrics and seeing the emotions of those dancing the tango proves the point: the Argentinians are a passionate people. But passionate people exist everywhere, and getting to know so many different nationalities on board a ship opens doors to that opportunity. The circumstance of growing up in various countries shapes the very core of humans. From the age of eight years old, Flo wanted to study in the United States. Her parents made education a priority, doing without a car and drilling into her the idea that "in our house, we persevere."

Everything has a balance. Although away from home, missing the benchmark events happening to the most important people in her life, Flo shared wonderful feelings of receiving a Christmas card each year from a satisfied guest met one day on a cruise. Ms. Belo says, "Whether at home or on the ship, you have to make [the experience] the best by saying, beyond fear, that you are proud. I am traveling, and now my new friends at sea are family. That's the thing that pulls me in the most."

chapter 4: non-stop memory making for kids

"How often does a six-year-old get to shoot hoops with nationally known characters?"

Cody Phillips, Assistant Manager, Adventure Ocean, USA

At the university, I wanted to be a professor, but I did a huge flop and taught summer sailing for six to seven-year-olds," says Cody, a newbie onboard *Allure of the Seas*.

Kids call Cody "Penguin"

"Only three percent of the crew are Americans, putting me in the minority. And of the first thirty friends I made on ship, none of them were Americans. On ships, you would think there would be a separation, but there is not. You look at someone's nametag just to wonder where are you from; what's your name? But it just gets blown out the window. Accents even get blown out the window. When you are home it's like where is that (accent) coming from? Here, you never hear the same accent. You get used to it instantly, and it's nice because it is a cultural melting pot, with the freedom of knowing that no one is judging other cultures, and that everyone has a voice. Good captains make the crew feel that everyone has a similar voice, whether you have three stripes or work in the galley. Here, you know, is one of the few places I've been in the world where there isn't that judgment. It's already on the table," comments Cody, manager for Adventure Ocean, the children's program.

Shaking hands with the lab's friendly skeleton

"The cultural nuances take a little time to absorb, like the elevator policies. In the states, you step aside for everyone getting out of the elevator before you get in. Having ten people, all trying to get in at the same time as those getting out, creates chaos. It's as if you were to bring a cultural melting pot together in different scenarios. Here, the crew has to live, work, eat, sleep, and do everything together so everyone has to adapt to each other's cultures. And, what other job allows you to meet 6,000 new guests every single week?"

Parents agree that children exhibit greater flexibility than adults. The different age groups deal with cultural diversity in opposite ways within their varying age groups, according to Cody. With the young ones, you get a ball, pen, or crayon in their hand in a group and it's a group function. They don't need to know each other's language. They all find comfort and commonality in that activity. Whether or not they speak the same language or have different skin tones gets lost the second they start turning to games.

Cody says, "It's refreshing. I know a lot of friends I grew up with are not culturally prepared, and they come visit me on a ship, and they get a little overwhelmed going to the mess and meeting a bunch of Filipinos or a bunch of people from Trinidad."

Brazilian guest having fun

Those fourteen-to seventeen-year-olds in the teen center have a different perspective, going through culture shock for the first time. Teens find comfort in the common areas of the dance floor or the social games at night. After a few days, they feel comfortable around each other. By day six, they walk around, laughing at each other's accents or tease about language issues. They take more time to bond, compared to the instant friendships developed with the three to eleven-year-olds.

Kids in shopping carts at the grocery, sitting in car seats in the McDonald's line, or waiting for food in restaurants, seem to have one thing in common: Nintendo DS. If you line a room in Adventure Ocean with thirty Nintendo games, Wiis, Xboxes, or computers, and you put thirty kids in that room and one ball in the middle of the floor, that ball will remain untouched, a sad commentary on the new form of socialization.

Exposure to science

Nearly every kid walks in with a DS hanging out of his back pocket. Kids even have their own Facebook account by the age of thirteen, a little overwhelming. Adventure Ocean has a creative activities program. Kids sign up for the programs because they see the Wiis in the windows, but rather than three-hour sessions of computers and electronic game time, the ship provides three hours of activities. They cut down the Nintendo time to fifteen minutes and then play games the rest of the session. By day five, those Wiis don't get turned on much. In the Voyagers room, the nine-to-eleven-year-olds still love the Wiis. A common phrase heard in the beginning of the cruise is "Do you want to play Tommy Hawk or Smash Brothers?" (Both are electronic games.) By the end of the week, that phrase changes to "Let's play a game of gaga ball!" (Name for a type of dodge ball from Israel.)

Cody explains, "You are removing them from what they know back home like hopping in the car for their ride home from school and turning on their DS. Or going home and getting a snack and flipping on a television show. Now, maybe they want to go home and play a game of gaga ball. I've known kids that I met a year ago, and they come back and say, 'Oh man, I like gaga ball. I can't wait. And we are playing it back in school, and I taught everyone how to play penguin madness.' They brought the games home so, hopefully, it will keep happening, and there is a movement toward anti-technology, so the kids don't get their iPhone, which explains it exactly. I mean, living the world via television. Some (children) don't know how to interact outside the classroom. They know how to get online, to sign on to Xbox live, to chat with friends, and text."

Learning about bugs

I, as the interviewer, shared a story about my children growing up in the country on a lake with plenty of room for soccer, sprinklers to run through, trees to climb, and forts to build. My son admitted that his friends wanted to play Nintendo when they came over, and I told him that maybe he needed to teach them how to play outside. Cody told a similar story of having ten acres to ride horses, chase snakes, build bike ramps, and play kickball in school tournaments. He explained that children come here who have never gotten sweaty from running in an open field. They have a lot of pent-up energy. Parents put on the forms that the kids take Ritalin or Conserta and that the crew needs to watch their children because they have ADHD.

Cody says, "Yeah, they might not listen as well as the others. But they are going to play the game. They need to run around, get sweaty, get exhausted. Maybe they do need that, and need to see there is a chance for them, and there is an area for them to excel. [They can be excited because they learned on the ship that] that they rocked at science, or that they could build a massive fortress. So there you go, future scientist, architect, or future baseball player. They might not get that [normally] because they are shot down day after day. We are like their best buddies, that older brother or sister who can show them this is cool, and they can be who they want to be."

In Adventure Ocean, an altercation could arise between the kids because, "He took my ball!" The intense argument doesn't get hot enough to pull the two kids apart. Cody tells the kids, "'We have a game to play, so you can either play the game or go sit in a corner and sulk.' That one thought usually turns the smiles back on with, okay, we are done with it."

Everyone asks silly questions. In Adventure Ocean, the staff members encourage this by putting silly notions in the children's heads on the first day.

Everyone has a nickname, including Cody, known as "Penguin" to the children. The nametag "Cody: United States" stays at his desk. His team includes Snowflake, Big Mamma, and Cheese.

Geology lab

"I'm a big storyteller," Cody says. "We want to be characters for these kids, because when they step into the room: goodbye parents. They don't get the opportunity very much to evolve. Imagination, strictly imagination. That is my foundation when I am in the room. Whether the kid is three or eleven, I am going to be wacky. With the three-year-olds, we have a friend called Fuzz Buzz. He is our alien friend who came down to the ship, and we are going to go look for him. Give me fifteen minutes with any age group, and they will want to meet Fuzz Buzz. All of a sudden, these kids are telling their parents Fuzz Buzz likes ice cream, and we need to go with our group detectors, these paper hats we made. I can't get off the ship without it. Later that evening the parents come back on board and say they weren't able to get the stupid group detectors off their kids' heads, and they wouldn't get into the water without it. In St. Thomas, they are asking the vendors, 'Have you seen Fuzz Buzz?'"

"With the nine-to-eleven-year-olds, we have them calling each other funny nicknames, and that is a really tough age group because it is right before teenage preadolescence with hormonal changes.

So, some think they are too cool for school, and we try to dissolve that and give them a really fun environment to goof off in where they are not going to be judged by the bully. There are no bullies, no popular kids, no shy guys. It's just one environment, one imaginative environment."

The staff for Adventure Ocean sees their share of beautiful children, all with their own little habits and situations. The bathroom scenarios entertain Cody's team. A little Russian boy about three years old, who spoke Russian and English fluently, fully potty-trained, went into the bathroom one day, and the staff kept hearing this noise like, *Ahhhhhhh.* They called in to him, and he responded with another *Ahhhhhhh.* Finally, the staff went in to check. The little boy asked for a book and then said, "Just gimme a minute." He said he just needed something to read and a minute or two. How ridiculous, the staff thought, that a three-year-old would ask for reading material and a minute. His parents came, heard the noise, and commented that this sounded like their son and they cracked up with laughter.

Americans eat about 18 acres of pizza every day.

Cody told another story about a little boy, about five, who thought he was Woody, the cowboy character from the movie, *Toy Story*. He wore the same cowboy outfit every day, and he didn't want to go anywhere on the ship except Adventure Ocean. He would come with his little rope and chase everyone around like cattle, and he would literally rope the kids. Every day, he would put on a rodeo show. In his mind, for those fifteen minutes, he became a rodeo clown. He went around the room performing his horse act, and then at the end, he would run face-first into a padded pillar. He would just run straight at it and knock himself down. All the children and parents knew him only as Woody.

Cultural differences reveal themselves in the teen center, the children's staff members report. In the three-to-eleven-year-old group a child might ask about that funny thing on your head or, "Why are you wearing that?"

That is awesome, Cody reports. Their attitude? Let us go play and not wait around for an answer. It's not in their head to think, "What do other people think?" like the thoughts of a teenager.

More often, the staff has to worry about the differences in how children from other cultures have been taught to play ball. American, British, and Canadian kids have been known to throw balls aggressively at other children's heads. It is also interesting to note that children of some cultures actually take a step back when they don't want to be touched by other kids. Each culture has different standards for closeness and personal space, and the staff keeps this in mind when problems arise among the children based on these differences.

Staff members encourage the children to stay together by asking them to hold hands while in line, but children from some eastern European cultures are not comfortable with the idea of holding other children's hands. They ask, "Why are you holding my hand?" But if a child doesn't feel comfortable, then they do not need to comply with the hand-holding rule. The child makes his own decision, but eventually, by the end of the week, he or she may well go from being the reserved one to being one who throws the ball too hard at other players.

The word "homesickness" doesn't appear in Cody's vocabulary. As a child, his parents preached the words, "The world's a much bigger place. Go out and see it." They wanted him to meet other cultures. His mother conquered the hurdles of moving to Hawaii as a child, but his father never had the opportunity to move around.

Cody says, "I miss more about the ship when I am home, than when I am on the ship and miss my home! I like the fast-paced living. Go, go, go.

I barely have enough time to sit down and catch my breath. For a lot of people, stress is a problem, but I guess my high functioning ADHD operates well in this world.

I like knowing that I can get a phone call at any time of the day or an alarm in the middle of the night or, when working with a child, get another call from the teen center with questions, or have to run down to my manager's office to get something about Make-a-Wish Foundation. Or, man, I am hungry and need to run to the mess, or guess what? I am in Rome today and better not miss that tour, but I have to be back by 3:00 p.m. or I will miss the ship."

"I was on Ritalin for a few years with a very small dosage and changed to Adderall at fifteen years old. I stopped taking it at twenty-two, and the only difference I notice is that I get tired more often if I am just sitting and not talking.

Here I'm moving every hour, every minute of my day 'cause I am responsible for 2000 children plus thirty staff and myself. Yeah, I put myself last on the list, but I get my food, plus I haven't been sick once while on the ship, so that must say something about how I take care of myself."

Just trying to keep up with Cody stretches your endurance. He certainly proves that high-energy kids can grow up to manage a staff and weekly waves of active kids.

Royal Caribbean International and its guests love Cody, and he loves them. What a pattern for the world to emulate as the next generation learns the joy of inter-cultural contacts and understanding.

chapter 5: the show floats on

"I remember the second night on board the ship, I was sitting in the crew mess and on one side somebody was eating fish heads and on the other they were eating pig's feet."

Gareth Smith, Production Manager, UK

"Working on the cruise ship is like working in a little town," says Gareth Smith, production manager. "If you need parts, you just pick up the phone and two minutes later you have an engineer, and in two more minutes, you have an electrician. In less than twenty-four hours, a new handmade part arrives. If a costume rips during a performance, the theatre department calls on their seamstresses. Especially during the Aqua show, with all the water, the costumes need repair on a daily basis.

Some 80,000 umbrellas are lost annually in the London Underground.

If I need extra hooks for the theatre, I call, and they make parts on the spot. At home [in the UK], or on tour, I might have to ring for a part and not receive it for two weeks."

Big difference between working on land and on sea. Engine, electrical, and deck departments all work together no matter if on the marine or hotel side. Operating on land consists of working with people from the same country who speak the same language.

Gareth says, "Everybody speaks English one way or another. Most of the electricians who work for me are Croatian. It took me a little time to adapt to the language but you get used to how they ask for things, how they say things. Yes, they'll [digress] into their own language, but I just go with it, and then they break down what they're saying to your level [of understanding]. They don't baffle you with science. It's quite amazing how everybody will just pull together and sort things out."

The turnaround of people coming and going in the theater department includes those on medical leave, compassionate leave, vacation, and those transferring to and from other ships. A hundred to a hundred-fifty people come and go weekly. The theatre department, affected by weekly turnaround, is usually notified of those who will return. If a new member comes aboard, management integrates each very carefully into the least important of the three venues on board, such as the Studio B ice rink, and builds their skills up from there. Only the most experienced performers end up in the Aqua Show, the most difficult venue on the ship.

View from the high dive platform [notice author below/center!]

Gareth points out the realities of adjusting to the food, "It can't just be lasagna, chips, and peas every night. How do I deal with the situation? When you've got nowhere else to go, then you have to eat what's offered]."

Gareth remembers the first week at sea. "After only a few weeks, I got used to the food. You know what tastes good and what you can't eat."

Adaptability: the middle name for managers and crew members alike. For those newbies who show signs of a closed-minded attitude, the motto of those more experienced is just to show them the right way, how to adjust.

The entertainment side of the ship gets its energy by finishing the show. Excitement at the end of the show makes one ready for the next day and the next challenge.

The Aqua show has a fast-paced tempo. The Aqua Theater, the world's largest amphitheater at sea, has a seventeen-foot-deep pool aft side. Huge wind sails behind the stage help protect divers from sudden gusts impacting their graceful Olympic-style dives off the fifty-foot, or seventeen-meter-high, dive platforms.

Gareth supervises Aqua Theater rehearsal

Most of the divers have competed in the Olympics. Acrobats perform both in the air, off a trampoline into the water, and on a moving stage that magically disappears underwater. Just minutes before this stage submerges, performers startle the crowd by walking across the water.

Backlit fountains provide more than just a synchronized backdrop of rain and mist. A nine-time world champion cliff diver states that waves break the water's surface tension, which softens the impact of his dives. Diving puts tremendous stresses on your body, so performers engage in acrobatics early in the dive to give their bodies time for proper positioning for water entry. Jumping in a straight vertical line from twenty feet or six meters, performers will enter the water at twenty-five mph or forty kph, an impact strong enough to compress the spine, break bones, or cause a concussion. Landing on the surface of the water like a pancake, flat, would cause injuries in the same way landing flat on concrete would. Water does not compress well due to the shape of its molecules and how they line up under pressure. By entering the water hands first, as performers do when they dive, you do not displace as much water as you would in a belly flop. When you dive, there is a gradual displacement of water around your hands and then a little more around your body, and if you watch the timing of the fountains carefully, you will see that as the diver performs the acrobatics in air, the fountains break the surface tension of the water. But timing is everything, and those moments put the production manager on edge. Parts of the audience look up, which catches everyone's attention, especially the thrill seekers as they watch the couple flying overhead. Suddenly the woman falls toward the audience until her body motion stops as her partner maintains a tight hold of her wrist.

"The man and woman doing tricks on the high wire flying over the audience are pretty safe," says Gareth, "but when performers are over the water, you don't know how performers are going to act."

Years of training qualify these actors for performing, but if dropped in an unusual way, they may hesitate. People have to move to the right place when pulled out of the water, or they can take a curtain with them. As far as acrobatics in the water are concerned, the manager works very closely with the bridge, ringing them up every hour before the show for weather conditions. Rain means the show goes on, but no audience will appear. Winds can be handled by the wind sails behind the stage. But even one degree of list can cause water issues, like water pouring out of the pool. Listing is when a ship leans to one side due to weather conditions, a computer glitch, or human error. Cruise ships list a lot so they can withstand heavy waves.

At the stage, four people stay underwater at all times. The movement of the boat forces them to move side to side constantly. Two can talk to the manager and the other two only listen with underwater devices. The manager operates from his office on deck twelve during the show, communicating with the people in the water through the pool system, listening to spot cues, and making sure the lights function properly (meaning the divers' green light works on cue), and the stage submerges when somebody dives into the water. The four in the water follow orders from the director watching that all goes well with the water levels. Getting through the shows without injury gives everybody on the team the excitement to go forward for the rest of the week. The Aqua show has fourteen nationalities working side by side, adapting to each other's customs and performing in sync with a moving ship under constantly changing weather.

chapter 6: rugby's #1 fan

"I've been thinking for a long time, if I could get all of the people and friends I have met in one place at the same time, it would be heaven."

Henri Tredoux, Asst. Executive Housekeeper, South Africa

Watching the television series *Love Boat*, Henri Tredoux, assistant executive housekeeper, fell in love with the idea of working on a cruise ship. Of his eleven years working in the hospitality industry, seven years have included cruise ship work. Meeting people of so many nationalities, he experienced doors opening all around the world. As a South African, Henry does not pay taxes on his income. Not paying taxes and having travel opportunities far outweighs any land-based job he ever had. He admits it takes a while to overcome the disadvantage of working so many months before returning home. But at home, he has two full months to do whatever he wants.

South Africa's biggest Rugby fan

Turnover due to crew's comings and goings makes management difficult because it feels like a continuous training process. By starting each new recruit's training with an open mind, Henri explains, he quickly learns to broaden his horizons.

Henri says, "I took my patches off little by little, which helped me adapt. Accepting that you have to do the same training over and over again, with different nationalities coming in with unique ways of doing things, closes the gap between you and them. You build up some great friendships and, unfortunately, at times, you have to let go of some. Don't take things personally as the other person may not have meant it that way."

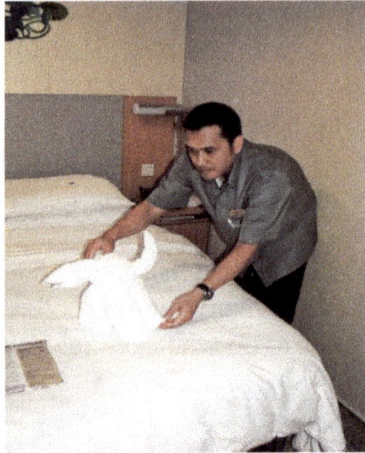

Bed time greeting

Having too many shipmates of the same culture on board breaks down the system.

For example, in housekeeping, too many Caribbean natives or Asians can encourage that particular group to stick together and to influence one another while not branching out and helping staffers of other cultures.

When you have a greater mix of nationalities, people tend to come out of themselves and push each other to achieve. If your work in your comfort zone with your *paisanos* (as we call our fellow countrymen, or good friends) on ship, then you tend to relax because they will support you and even help with your work duties. Diversity creates competition or friendly rivalry.

Cruise ship employment offers various opportunities for fun. Shopping, one of Henri's favorite pastimes in the quaint little island shops, builds anticipation for the next port of call. In the beginning, the enticing souvenirs like Mexican sombreros filled his room and luggage.

Now he looks to browse hidden alleyways for treasures and tasty treats. Off ship and back home, his guiding light, rugby, entertains him sometimes twenty-four hours a day.

South Africa has 80% of Africa's rail infrastructure.

In nineteenth-century England, people viewed sports as a key element in the development of students. Two distinct patterns developed: the handling versus the kicking type of playing ball. The kicking game dominated the ball-game scene and became known as the sport of football.

Status and fame drove competition to a fierce level between colleges. The three colleges, Winchester, Harrow, and Rugby, divided themselves between those favoring the kicking style or the handling style of ball games.

Rugby College in central England led the way in favoring the handling style. Legend tells the story of a student named William Webb Ellis in 1823 picking up the ball and running with it, "showing a fine disregard for the rules of football," according to the story. The beginning of rugby football, some say. The World Cup, presented to the winner of the Rugby World Championships every four years, carries his name, the William Webb Ellis Cup. While Rugby College enthusiastically spread their version of football code rules using the handling style for football, confusion reigned as to which style of rules the schools should adopt.

In 1863, meetings to unify both styles into one single version failed. British nineteenth-century colonizers and entrepreneurs spread the resulting news of both sports surviving, one as Rugby Union football (rugby) and the other as the Association of Football (soccer).

Rugby, a religion, as they say in South Africa, begins when one takes his first step. Every boy grows up wanting to wear the official team colors of gold and green (of the half-million registered rugby players, women account for ten thousand).

The assistant executive housekeeper on a cruise ship begins the day at 7:00 a.m. with a quick briefing among supervisors discussing the issues of the day.

Three assistant housekeepers manage the housekeeping department, with Henri tackling the seventeenth floor down to deck ten, another taking deck ten to deck three, and a third taking care of the back of the house (laundry, staff, and officers' rooms).

The crew replaces linens frequently. Managers receive dozens of e-mails from the numerous departments on board with messages to supervisors of special requests from guests or urgent organization needed somewhere.

Lunchtime precedes what the employees call the international naptime.

The majority of crew work in the early morning; they take a nap between two and five, and then get back to work again.

High standards for care

Three sets of laundry are in constant motion. They rotate sets on Sunday and Wednesday on the seven-night cruise. One of three sets remains in the staterooms, while another sits in carts in the laundry, waiting for washing, and the third rests neatly on shelves after going through the pressing machine. Yes, they iron the sheets!

How long do sheets last? Because of chemicals and the quality of the water, sheets last about eighteen months. Crew members restock about a thousand new sheets monthly because of wear, tear, and stains. The order goes down to the inventory manager, and he checks the huge storage area on board for linens as well as toiletries (like bath tissue and shampoo), and places the order. That order comes out of the housekeeping budget. He reorders as needed, and the cycle starts all over again.

Five supervisors work under each assistant housekeeping manager with twenty stateroom attendants handling approximately ten rooms each. The twelve runners take the linens to the two linen keepers. The seventeen stateroom attendants at the back of the house rotate every two weeks. Guests' ratings determine whether they keep working on the floors with their guests or at the back of the house. The lowest seventeen of those working upstairs take the place of those working the back of the house, which keeps them all on their toes. Women make up about twenty-seven percent of the housekeeping staff.

People come to cruise lines from around the world to enjoy a getaway. Guests appreciate a cruise ship with crew members representing seventy-nine nationalities because this offers those foreign guests the opportunity to speak with someone using their own language, and makes following directions to the library or a quiet place to sit and have a glass of wine a lot easier.

chapter 7: green thumbs afloat

"Guests feel like they are in their own backyard."

Gelashe Cui Javier, Landscape Specialist, Philippines

When a cruise line transplants a city to the ocean, the job descriptions become sophisticated. The crew originates from different cultures, as we have learned, but will Royal Caribbean International have to search for a landscaper? After studying and majoring in plant science in school, Gelashe Javier worked one year (1994) for a landscaping company in the Philippines in charge of five hotels.

Creative landscape architecture

During the next eight years, Mr. Javier maintained the indoor and outdoor landscapes for the Hotel Peninsula, Manila. Royal Caribbean International came to the Philippines looking for a horticulturist for their ship, *Grandeur of the Seas*, and found Gelashe. When the opportunity came about for him to move to Finland to work with the designer of the landscaping for *Allure of the Seas*, Gelashe couldn't resist the temptation.

The brand-new *Allure of the Seas* arrived in Fort Lauderdale on November 11, 2010, ready for the establishment of tropical gardens in the central park. The affluent ambience of the 21,000-square foot, open-air, exotic garden would fill the gap between the ship's split superstructures.

Loving care for plants

Originally, the fifth deck design opened to the sky. All the rain, and possible hurricanes bringing high winds, put a damper on that idea, giving way to the new concept of putting a roof over the promenade of deck five, creating a space for a central park with tropical gardens opening to the sky. A tiled pathway meanders in and out of garden beds, private restful seating alcoves, and trendy restaurants.

Originally, the executives and design team wanted mounds of grass in the middle of the central open area to create a New York Central Park effect. Visions of passengers sitting in the grass with picnic lunches on blankets filled their heads.

After much discussion, they settled on the current very successful plan with Central Park displaying its meandering paths and restaurants or shops on either side.

After Royal Caribbean International gave the contractor four days to install the 12,178 plants, the contractor offered a more realistic time budget of three weeks, still time to have *Allure of the Seas* ready for its first departure on December 5, 2010.

The contractor hired workers to install the plants, including having crew members pitch in whenever possible to get the job done in an unbelievable four days prior to the first sailing.

A five-story wall of plants

An established root system would help some of the more fragile plants begin their lives away from land with a better guarantee of longevity. The trees and plants, like the ground cover, Liriope, started their growth spurts six weeks before coming aboard the ship. The ship's entrances were not large enough to accommodate the arrival of over twenty-foot tall trees, so cranes dropped the fifty-six trees over the seventeenth deck down onto deck eight. Ninety-six species of trees, with only one fruit-bearing tree, the mango, thrive in their environment with attention given to their needs at least twice daily, sometimes more often. Curved planters line the walkways filled with varying sizes of aluminum containers. The designer took into consideration the variables of plant life existing on the floating hotel confined to aluminum pots versus thriving in the freedom of rich soil.

"If plants die while out to sea, they are not replaced in Jamaica or Mexico. We have one supplier in Fort Lauderdale who sells us plants previously treated and tested for insects.

"We are in close contact with the Department of Agriculture, monitoring the plant life for insects and disease. Every two weeks two officers from the Department of Agriculture come aboard and check the plants randomly for insects. If they find certain types of insects, they respond with the appropriate action.

"We have three different colors of sticky paper, blue, yellow, and white, that we randomly place on plants and trees once a week. Fruit flies or any other unknown varieties of insects get caught on the paper.

"At the end of the cruise each week, we take the paper off the plants and trees and collect them for the Department of Agriculture to check for [problem] insects. If there are insects that the Department objects to, they let us know, so we can have an insect-free environment," says Gelashe.

Trimming 12,000 plants keeps him busy

Temperature change poses the greatest problem for the plants. From Fort Lauderdale to the Caribbean, and down to Mexico, huge variances occur in temperatures and humidity.

High winds also pose problems. Although three hours of direct sunlight sounds perfect for plant growth, tropical heat makes it necessary to mist the plants to keep the leaves from burning.

Smoke eaters disguised as art. In 10 minutes, they can clear smoke

Three horticulturists monitor the plants daily, including the living wall, a five-deck-high facade of greenery.

Drip system irrigation nourishes the plants with liquid fertilizer the first three months, and then time-released fertilizer feeds the plants a healthy diet through pipes weaving under leaves and around tree trunk bases.

The pressurized pipes control the amount of water fed to the plants every day for twenty minutes.

The taller trees and areas needing more than the twenty minutes get tender care with manual soakings from crew members. The architect chose a mix of species selected for their ability to survive in the geographical areas in which the ships sail.

Plants around the park include the Bleeding-Heart Vine, Black Olive Tree, White Striped Tasman Flax Lily, Gamboge Tree, Kalanchoe, Sun Parasol, Lady Palm and Snake Plant.

About forty-six planter beds house 2000 individual aluminum modules holding the 12,000 plants, trees, vines and flowers. As the plants mature, they will become bigger and more beautiful. Trees will eventually stretch to two decks high and vines will burst with flowers.

"We have birds visiting us regularly as we dock at the various ports. Sometimes a bird will come aboard in Haiti, stay three days, and fly off in Jamaica. I monitor the bird sounds we pipe into the speaker system so the sounds feel natural and not too loud," Gelashe proudly explains.

Philippines has the largest diaspora network in the world with 11 million overseas.

An orange butterfly found the Jasmine winding its way toward the sun along a supportive lamppost. He didn't mind my taking his picture and I wondered if he would find his way back to Haiti today before the ship left the dock. The best opportunity for seeing butterflies on board comes quickly after docking in St. Marten, near a butterfly farm there. For some reason, they like the smells and colors of *Allure of the Seas* gardens. They fly all the way over the seventeen decks and down into the gardens of deck eight.

"Sometimes guests ask me personal advice on how to propagate a plant or what kinds of plants grow best in their own areas. Once a man told me all of his tropical gardens died over winter. When the landscape specialist asked him where he lived, he replied, 'New York!' Everyone laughed. 'Maybe you need to put in a rock garden," Gelashe, the specialist, replied.

Gelashe says, "I didn't expect to work again in a big garden after leaving Manila. The idea of the central park garden theme provides a peaceful and re-laxing place [for guests] while out at sea, especially in the afternoons and eve-nings."

Musicians, playing the violin or guitar, entertain those strolling or relaxing in overstuffed chairs under the shaded sitting areas or the stars.

Imagine a day where you visit with people from many cultures, or sip a bev-erage of choice just outside Chops (a gourmet restaurant) while watching birds, butterflies, and exotic plants in the middle of the ocean as you delight to a live concert featuring a Brahms trio softly blending with your conversation.

Thank Royal Caribbean International and Gelashe for their vision and skills in creating this paradise on earth!

✿ chapter 8 : keep crews smiling

"We celebrate the diversity!"

Berdy Bishop, HR Officer, South Africa

"How long is a piece of string? I guess it depends on what presents itself," Berdy, a South African said, when asked to summarize her role as a human resources executive officer.

"Custodian of organizational policies," describes her role, a position of far-reaching responsibilities. Striking a balance between managing people, and conducting the cruise business in accordance with legal requirements, means acting not only as a caretaker, but also as a protector.

The growth factor which includes more ships, larger ships, more hired staff and more customers has added a completely different dimension to Royal Caribbean International.

Diverse issues on a day-to-day basis present themselves, whether they involve managers, crew members, or appropriate fair labor practices. The unconventional schedule of duties takes away the nine-to-five scenario, giving managers the opportunity to see crew members working even at midnight.

South Africa is the second largest exporter of fruit in the world.

Hiring involves a screening process that starts with global hiring partners who act as agents for Royal Caribbean International for sourcing a potential work force. Initially, crews display their verbal communication abilities in English, whether basic or advanced. Literacy and job specific skills may involve different screening and assessment processes according to the rank of the job.

A representative for the company does the interviewing of the finalists after they complete the initial screening process. Shore-side groups develop the training programs, gathering input from the various managers within the fleet who understand the skills necessary to fulfill the various positions.

Training managers understand the dynamics of cultural diversity and problem-solving techniques. Several training managers will work onboard, executing the training along with the safety officer, security officer, and environmental officer. The training and development managers focus predominantly on values, ethics, new hires, leadership training, cultural diversity, and other organizational needs.

In the United States, one seldom finds as much diversity in cultures from every corner of the globe as in Royal Caribbean International's fleet of ships.

The world can learn from this work schedule and integration, especially the United Nations! Here, none of life's issues divide into black or white, good or bad, in or out. Cultural traits and customs, deeply embedded in people from birth, provide myriad ways of thinking, seeing, and hearing.

Takes pride in the universal culture

Gestures, including movements of the hands, face, or body, convey very different meanings depending on social or cultural settings.

The significance of the same gesture could range from complimentary to highly offensive in different countries. The smile, the most common facial expression in the world, can give conflicting messages depending on which nationality gives or receives it.

Russians consider a smile, given freely to strangers (as we Americans do), as impolite or strange. In Asia, a smile can signify embarrassment, while the Scandinavians consider showing emotion, like a smile, as a weakness.

Imagine the confusion when a crew member from Bulgaria or the Middle East moves his head up and down as to signal "no" while smiling.

The rest of the world uses that movement to signal yes! Connecting the thumb and forefinger in a circle and holding the other fingers straight signals "okay" or "everything's fine" for most of the world, but not if one lives in Iran or certain parts of Latin America where that sign is offensive. Touching, hugging, kissing on the cheeks, or even touching the head of a child, could signal a violation of one's private space in some societies.

Nonverbal communication includes the use of physical space. Both Americans and Europeans demand more space to satisfy their comfort levels than

Middle Easterners or Latin Americans. The latter might ask, "Why do you stand so far from me?" The former might ask, "Why do you stand so close?"

One of the more noticeable differences between nationalities, with nonverbal communication occurring 'round the clock, is eye contact. Latin Americans and Americans consider not looking someone in the eye as suspicious or disrespectful behavior.

Yet, prolonged eye contact in some Asian countries symbolizes disrespect.

Learning in advance about cultures and methods of nonverbal communication can save one embarrassment and many misunderstandings

When asked, "Are there challenges with effective communication for the management team of Royal Caribbean International when hiring new crew members?" (Called new hires).

Berdy answered, "You would think that! And that would be my paradigm when I came into the organization. That is what I geared myself up for, like it's going to be mission critical to do this.

Despite having seventy-nine nationalities, that is not really an obstacle. It might take some people a little longer to grasp something, certainly when you are relaying information about how critical it is to work together as we all do in this world, as well as with acronyms and that kind of thing. I think because people work and live together, there is a lot of interaction between individuals, so they get to know each other very quickly and they are incredibly accepting of each other.

It would be naive of me to bring everybody in and believe everybody will be happy. You will have people who don't adapt to the environment and they move on.

But, by and large, the greater majority does get along. The common denominator is they want to work here. Because we do the training, understanding diversity even in all our own interactions, we never focus on slanting something in a particular direction.

"We celebrate diversity. And it is an inclusive environment. I deal with very few situations at all that relate to cultural conflict. Honestly, you might venture into the social norms, but that would be more like how men approach women or women approach men. Here it is concentrated. They are together all day and all night."

Berdy summarized the guest situation this way. Many guests sail on a specific ship because a crew member offers such remarkable service.

Countless letters arrive describing the level of service a crew member extended during a guest's visit. Crew members extending that courtesy become a part of those guests' lives.

Sometimes those relationships develop from an adverse situation. Guests cruise for many reasons, like escaping an unfortunate situation. Sometimes guests must deal with emergencies while on board, and because of the friend-ship and support the crew provides, they remain friends.

Based in the United States, Royal Caribbean International follows the proce-dures and protocols of the United States. The second tier to that is the synergy in regulations required by US law for a company operating in the United States as well as Royal Caribbean International's flag state of the Bahamas, which has its own requirements.

Berdy says, "It's demanding. There are no two ways about that. But it also takes on its own life form because you almost have different layers. You come on, depending on what your position is, and you are either going to be here four, six or eight months.

So you have that to begin with, and then you break it down, and you have what is the length of the cruise. Seven days is life for us, because we do a seven-day cruise. So, your energy will go around that seven days.

And then it's day one again and your energy builds around that. They (crew members) do start to pace themselves, particularly those who have been around for a while.

They will be sharing with each other how to go the distance, if you will. So, all the wait staff will talk to each other and encourage each other to keep it going.

But, again, very quickly one accepts that this is the environment. It doesn't stop and you know it. You're here for however long you are here.

"There is no day off. It doesn't exist, but you are fine with that. But people learn that as well, so when it's work, they work, and when it's down time, it's down time. If it's a port of call they enjoy, provided they are not on duty, they will be off the ship.

Alternately, they will head straight for the cabin and get a few hours' rest. That's why you have this afternoon lull. Generally, it's flat-out until lunch. Peo-ple maximize this [time] because they are probably going to go again until mid-night. So, it's this unwritten law where it's the afternoon siesta, if you will."

This dedicated crew member accepts the rhythm of the assignment and takes pride in this "universal" culture welded into a team from many nations on board.

chapter 9: 2704 hotel rooms + laundry

"You always can do something for somebody or somebody can do something for you."

Ivaylo Ivanov, Executive Housekeeper, Bulgaria

Staffing a ship designed with the luxury and amenities of a five-star hotel means finding people to head the department of "comfortability", meaning housekeeping. Ivaylo Ivanov, executive housekeeper, takes charge of 2,704 staterooms, suites, and accommodations, and oversees the laundry department.

Working on board changes a person

How many linens might his crew members process on this ship on a daily basis? It takes a great team to make sure the processing functions properly. Success or failure directly impacts the guests' experience in their accommodations. This well-structured department has three assistants, twelve supervisors, and a laundry master in charge of laundry operations. Twelve years in the hospitality industry gives Ivaylo the experience he needs on a daily basis. Three schools honored him with diplomas in hospitality, including the International College in Bulgaria (his home country), The International College in the Netherlands, and the Swiss Hotel Management School in Switzerland. After five years working for a five-star, five-diamond hotel in Beverly Hills, CA, he decided to try something different: cruise-ship work. With only two contracts behind him, he already loves the business.

Washes 200,000 pounds a week

Ivaylo says, "We are one family. It is so rewarding at the end of the day to ensure that everybody is looking in the same direction. It is challenging at certain points because we do have different nationalities. The policies and the procedures that are in place to ensure that there are very high levels of respect among the crew members is something unique. We have zero tolerance toward disrespect and to offensive behavior. Everybody brings a piece of experience, contributes to the team, and that makes it a diversified team. And when you apply a management style, you can gain so many different visions and ideas and then incorporate them, mix them up, then shape them and achieve great results."

Chef's uniforms ready for action

Cruise ships have an international guest pool. Hospitality encourages integration of many languages on every deck. The ship has a crew member database of languages spoken available to supervisors. Servicing a guest takes just one phone call. Crew member Ricardo speaks Portuguese. Two Brazilian guests come on board with little English skills, and suddenly Ricardo shows up with a "How are you?" in Portuguese. Anytime a language barrier presents itself, the stateroom attendant identifies the language and locates the international ambassador who speaks the language in order to help the guest. International ambassadors speak up to five languages and wear a nametag with flags representing the languages they speak.

Stateroom attendants distribute the *Cruise Compass*, each night as they turn down the beds. The *Cruise Compass* is the ship's daily newsletter, listing pages of helpful information that helps the guests have a better cruise experience. The attendant knows if he has a group of Italians, and he will make sure each of them will receive their *Compass* in Italian. With thousands of guests, crew members try to give the best service to each, including helping them understand the activities the ship offers on a daily basis.

Presses table linens and sheets

"On my first contract with Royal Caribbean International," Ivaylo recalls, "I was on board only two months and had the honor to present a service award to a stateroom attendant who celebrated thirty-five years with the company. I mean, if you worked in a company for thirty-five years, that means you were well taken care of. In the housekeeping division, most of my members have been with the company for five, ten, or fifteen years. That's your life, and you have dedicated your life to something. The company had just celebrated forty years and I said, 'Captain, could you, ever in your wildest dreams, imagine that something like this would exist? It's unbelievable.'"

Actually, including predecessor companies, Royal Caribbean International traces its business to 1968. "Every week," Ivaylo says, "I have been asked by a good percentage of guests if they can take their stateroom attendants back home with them. It is the connection.

We are the personal assistants of our guests. We are insuring that everybody is feeling comfortable in his or her home away from home. Many guests leaving say 'we will be back because of so-and-so helping us.' I would say we are doing a fantastic job in our ratio of returning guests. Amazing.

Pressed and folded sheets from pressing machine

"This is one thing that the guests laugh about, that there is so much attachment to crew members. There is also so much attachment to ship sizes. We do have guests for whom *Allure of the Seas* or *Oasis of the Seas* is not their cup of tea, because they do enjoy the ratio of the nice, sexy small ship with fewer passengers where they have more of a quiet experience. There are many options. That is why we [Royal Caribbean International] have so many different types of ships, so many classes. There is something for everybody.

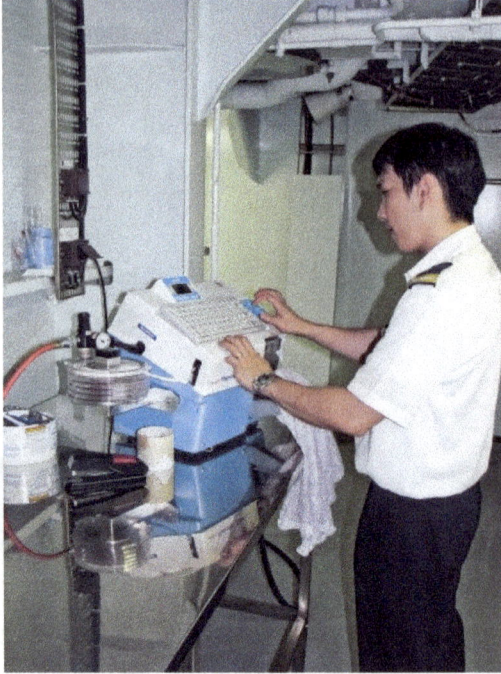

Pressing business

"When you are back in Europe, would you ever consider this cruise ship work? You can get exposed to so many different things working on a ship. Working in a land hotel on shore you will never ever get that exposure to cultures and [food] dishes."

"I observed at breakfast a couple eating Cornflakes," I said to Ivaylo. "That seems bland when choices include exotic fruits, dried fruits and nuts, egg dishes, varieties of meats and cheeses, dozens of pastries, and every kind of topping for oatmeal or yogurt."

In Bulgaria, you must lie to at least one person on the "day of the lie", April 1

Ivaylo commented, "We cannot help everyone to be so open-minded to different foods and experiences. But it is great that we have all those choices, and at the end of the day, everyone can go ahead and experience different options."

Dry bath towels

Most people would assume the busiest day of the week, embarkation, would stress Ivaylo. But disembarkation can lead to unexpected problems that require all involved to keep their sense of humor. Many guests choose to leave their luggage outside their stateroom door on the last night of cruise, so the staff can deliver it to the port, and the guest doesn't have to carry it ashore. Late on the last cruise night, a careful wife packed the suitcase to leave outside their door with all her husband's clothes. When he awoke, the suitcase was loaded on huge pallets and on its way ashore so his choice for clothing was towels or nothing. He chose towels. I hope that he went home with a smile.

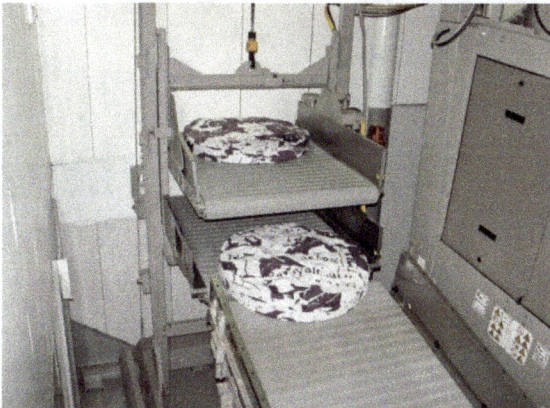
Pool towels on conveyor belt from washing machin

Loading dirty towels to conveyor to wash machine

5000 Pool Towels Folded Every Day

Working on a cruise ship changes a person. Not only will you become well-rounded and worldly, but you will come away with a better understanding of global problems, and the culture and way of life of people from around the globe.

🦅 chapter 10: leave the "campsite" clean

"Guests are consumers on a cruise but expect to see the beauty of an island without seeing waste created by their presence on land or sea."

Peter Roy, Environmental Officer, UK

"Cruise ships," says Peter Roy, "are all about seeing beautiful places. To enjoy food and drink and to do nothing they [guests] have to do at home. Its very nature is about consumption. Royal Caribbean International, over the last seven years, has upgraded its 'reduce, re-use and recycle' [the three watchwords of Royal Caribbean International] procedures."

Peter Roy, environmental officer, born in the United Kingdom, manages all environmental issues on the ship. "We don't throw anything overboard. I come from a government background, a recycling background, so [this job] was an easy fit for me. We've gone from about 1% recycling our first week to around 80% recycling, [and] it all goes on behind the scenes. The guests don't see it."

Allure of the Seas hopes by December to have the air, water, and power systems perform close to the highest possible ecological and recycling targets.

Whatever remains of waste besides the familiar items like aluminum cans, plastics, glass, batteries, and paper finds the incinerator. *Allure of the Seas* has two incinerators, operating with higher temperatures than any others on land do, so the stack spews mostly some steam and carbon dioxide. Particles of ash will get recycled and tested for contaminants. That method handles almost all dry waste.

More than 8,000 people use showers, sinks, and toilets. The state-of-the-art processing plant purifies the waste as it goes through the system to become cleaner and cleaner.

Eventually it produces liquid nearly resembling drinking water. But it isn't, and the ship does not aim to reduce it to drinking water! You pour it into a glass, it appears clear, and they put it overboard.

International rules do not exist for this procedure. Royal Caribbean International has searched the world for the highest standards to adopt, the strict rules used in Alaska.

Different AWP (Advanced Water Purification) systems have migrated to ships, but their rules apply to land use, and their recycling systems squeeze into smaller spaces. One of two systems handle kitchen waste. The ship discharges it overboard or dries it in the incinerator.

Wet kitchen waste would force an incinerator to consume large amounts of fossil fuel, so the ship usually discharges in deep oceans away from land.

Reduce, re-use, recycle: Peter Roy

"We don't discharge around any coastal areas because we have to be out twelve nautical miles, which in ecological terms is almost a desert in terms of nutrients.

So, if anything, we might be helping the marine life with free dinners, free fish food," says Peter.

Swimming pools follow a minimum monthly water replacement schedule, but generally flush more often due to "accidents." *Allure of the Seas* has mostly fresh water pools and one with salt water.

Even before they cut the steel for *Allure of the Seas*, their concept was to be as environmentally friendly as possible. The shape of the hull is such that it reduces resistance, using less fuel.

A special coating underneath the ship helps get the vessel through the water faster with the same amount of fuel. The environmental department uses incentives to drive down the use of fuel.

A friendly contest with sister ship *Oasis of the Seas* continues to see who has the best record for fuel and water consumption.

Find ice cream, hot dogs and a merry-go-round here

Peter Roy says, "We have a training program for the crew called Save the Waves. Every week we have about one hundred crew leaving and joining the ship, and they have some environmental training, so it is a challenge for me to meet and greet them [not knowing how much training they need].

We go through regulations and take them behind the scenes, and I show them a power-point presentation about the equipment. It can be a little bit of an information overload.

What happens is that we have constant reinforcement through a dedicated television crew channel for safety videos. We have drills constantly, and every crew member has a particular job or safety function.

Extending the environmental officer's job involves public health and awareness. Personal hygiene and hand washing stations exist everywhere."

One program outside the ship's duties helps keep the crew members busy during their time off, and the crew becomes involved in environmental projects.

Volunteers help with the Indian River Conservation Project in Florida. Locals bring buckets of oyster shells to the ship every week. Crew members come to a certain deck to work on thousands of shells, filling pallets, drilling a single hole in each shell. A cable tie is placed through the hole and then attached to a mat.

Over time, new oysters colonize the mat, which filters or purifies the water by removing contaminants. The crews also help to clean beaches and have other volunteer projects of this type.

Raising two teenagers, two dogs, and two cats, this sailor, Peter Roy, finds the sofa a popular place back home. Growing up with a ship captain for a father, Mr. Roy's life revolved around ex-pats from the far corners of the world.

Britain: the only country in the world without its name on postage stamps.

His father, born in India, moved to Tanzania where Peter Roy's spent his boyhood years. For Peter, his ten weeks on and ten weeks off means plenty of family time, helping with the chores, cleaning, and shopping. Peter says, "I have a Land Rover that's sixteen years old now, and I just like to jump in that and fill the environmentally friendly natural gas tank.

I've got two Labradors and, during the day when everyone is away working, that Land Rover gets me to places—like, you miss the smell of grass and trees and just being in the forest with different sounds, walking with nature.

We do occasionally travel and take off to South Africa. Fortunately, I have a family that understands. I used to think people would think, 'But you are traveling.' Yes, it's another port and another working day for us. But, after nine years of going around and around Cuba, those same ports of call, there is very little that I haven't seen. We have to remember it's a seven-day per week operation so we don't get any weekends off. If there is an issue in the middle of the night, you have to deal with it.

"I do like diving. That's something I indulge in when I am on the ships. All afternoon you will find the crew off the ship doing their thing, and with me, it is getting on a little boat and going off somewhere and getting wet. It's two or three hours and when you are in the water you just forget who you are. It's not relative and you are just concentrating on the moment."

When asked what Mr. Roy got homesick for besides family and friends, he said, "Being able to cook and being able to eat when I want to eat. I can't say the food is bad at all. You have your choice, but it's on a rotation so you will see the same things on the same days, week after week.

"With the 2,000 crew, I understand it is tricky and would require a lot of planning to change that. Of course, there are costs as well. One thing I really couldn't understand in my first contract was why some crew would get off the ship and go and eat. There is plenty of food on the ship.

And it's free. But the chance to sit down in a different location and eat different food and get waited on by someone else—I think psychologically that has got to help."

Clean oceans and beaches are an essential part of the cruise experience. Just as important is the protection of sensitive marine habits and wildlife. The cruise industry has a stake in protecting the ocean environment. New technologies help minimize the environmental impact from cruise ships.

chapter 11: having fun creating fun

"[When] coming to America, I was twenty-three. It was amazing for me to fly for a thirteen-hour flight over the ocean to Wal-Mart. I wouldn't say it was a culture shock but a cultural embrace."

Zack Stratford, Activities Manager, South Africa

"I've always been interested in design and how human beings operate in a space," states Zack, coming from an educational background of design and architecture back home. "And design is the passion of my life, and if the space is done correctly, human beings and their emotions are highly affected. So, if you [give] them a great space, they will be very happy. To work on ships involves a very tight space. While I was designing, I wanted to (A.) Work on ships to save money, so I could move to England and further my design career, and then (B.) At the same time, work and study while on board a cruise ship because you have limited space [my own cabin for quiet and privacy] and (C.) I watched Love Boat as a kid. There are always experiences to learn from. If life gives you lemons, make lemonade."

South Africa: one of 12 nations supplying drinkable tap water.

Zack feels the amount of energy and joy he gets from every single day totally outweighs the long workdays. He isn't rushing his dream to one day become cruise director; instead, he wants to step up the ladder, acquiring experience along the way. Zack's job as activities manager puts him in all areas of the ship, whether it be coordinating the men's belly flop contest or singing and dancing with the DreamWorks characters in the Aqua-theatre performance.

He says, "I believe it's beneficial to your team and to yourself, having experience and if you step up with confidence [moving to a higher job position]. Otherwise, if you get into position too quickly, sometimes throwing somebody in the deep end [of a new job with new responsibilities, it] teaches somebody how to swim, but it is very stressful and can be very damaging to your body and your team members. So, yeah, I am just enjoying the ride, the journey [gaining experience], because life is a journey at the end of the day."

Culture shock affects individuals differently. Many Americans and British come aboard and battle with the lack of creature comforts, the closeness of family life, limited space, and structured eating times. Vacation time usually means going home to family and friends for crew members. A two-month vacation offers plenty of time for catching up with family with time left over for sightseeing trips to places dreamed about while working those consecutive long days. Coming back from vacation, where you can explore nature, and enjoy home-cooked food and fresh water, into fluorescent lights, different sleeping patterns, work schedules, and desalinated water takes the staff about two weeks to really settle back into and accept. Sometime a crew member thinks about giving up.

Zack Stratford on the job

"Please don't do that," Zack advises. "Just stick out the two weeks; by then you'll find your groove, and you'll get into it. If you enjoy it, you'll come back for four or five hundred more months. But if you don't enjoy it, then it's not for you, and there is something else for you in life. It's not as if you failed. It's just a big adjustment."

Life at sea perfects life skills starting with the "ten-foot policy." If you are ten feet away from a person, you acknowledge them with a smile; at a distance of four feet, you greet them. A simple 'good morning,' 'good afternoon,' or 'lovely day' makes for a beautiful environment. Smiling is habit-forming. When walking down the street while on vacation, and off the boat, a crew member putting the ten-foot policy to work catches strangers by surprise. Land people are not used to such friendliness, but the response is always positive.

When Zack was back at home, the teller in the bank window didn't acknowledge him for over twenty seconds so he moved to the next window. His mother reminded him that he was not on the ship and to calm down. Zack's mother has learned all about the ship. She's applied the ten-foot policy to her hairdresser business. Even in the small details, like serving tea and cakes, she has seen a difference in her profitability and clientele.

Zack has told his mother, "If I ever find myself making business on land, then ninety-five percent of that business knowledge I will have learned aboard the ship."

He continues, "For me, life is a cycle, with small ones and big ones [experiences]. Once you realize this, you do your best job, the people get happy, and you get happy, and the ratings [customer reviews at the end of the cruise week] are good.

The guests have more enthusiasm when they approach the activities on the ship, which means they give you more energy as a host, meaning you have more fun and can do a better job, and the cycle just gets bigger and bigger [people being happy].

The gentleman in the head office said we have the world's largest cruise ship, and we have the best hardware, like the LED screens in the Aqua-theatre. Now we need the software to match, and that is the staff, and the way they approach the situations, how they host activities, and manage them.

So that is my driving force. That's what I love about Royal Caribbean International and wish the earth and the world could take more of a stand like that, but obviously, we can't fire you from your life. Effective communication comes with time.

Tell a Polish, Jamaican, or Indian person that the sky is blue and all will perceive the idea in a different way. Nationalities respond differently to coaching and communication, which gives the managers the responsibility of determining who have the stronger personalities versus the timid crew needing a little more tender hand holding."

Land people have more interaction with their families than crew members, who work for months without seeing family members. But, when crew members return home, they may find a sister who lives above her parents in a duplex and only sees those parents once a month, perhaps when coming or going to work. At the same time, the crew member spends so much time with his/her parents, they can get annoyed at times.

Flying high on the ocean

Most crew members miss family and friends while on the ship, but, what do they miss when off the ship?

"I love my two lives. It's great," Zack says. "But what I miss about the ship are the spontaneous breakfasts, lunches, and dinners in the mess hall. They have these big round tables that seat eight, and I always sit at one of those because I need more space and I am always busy working, and because I know people are gonna sit down who have different nationalities. And the part I love the most is you always can speak to somebody. There will be at least three different cultures from around the world that you can have a meal with.

There is no place in the world where this happens as frequently as it does here on the ships. We always start talking about what we do at home. We always have these theme nights in the dining hall. That spurs conversation like, 'Oh, what do you eat when it's your Christmas?' Like for me, Christmas is in the summer, and we go to the beach and have a BBQ. Some have a white Christmas, and that is a polar opposite for me and brings an entire different culture. So, I find it so fascinating, and generally at the dinner table they always talk about the guests, and I always change the conversation to speak more about National Geographic topics."

The captain has his top ten weekly best questions asked by guests. Next to a sign on the steps that says to Deck Five, a passenger asks, "Do these stairs take me to deck fourteen?" One of Zack's favorite questions asked was, "Do these stairs go up and down?" to which Zack responds to the guest that it depends on which way you walk.

Zack recalls one gentleman who asked the best question Zack had heard in a long time. As the guest disembarked from the gangway, he asked, "Do you know of any good hotels in the area?"

"Yes," Zack replied, "It has a nice pool and a nice day place."

The gentleman asked, "And to stay for the night?"

Zack said, "Do you want to come back later when you finish the cruise?"

"No, I want to check in for the night."

Zack smiled with, "Do you know we are sailing away today?"

Royal Romance offers to organize wedding plans, but sometimes the little things, like a marriage proposal, get an added boost from the staff. Zack remembers a couple who had cruised before on the same ship. The couple walked the deck at sunset, watching the ship leave port.

Suddenly, a violin player appeared (his arrival arranged by the fiancé). The violinist began playing, and oblivious to the setup, the girl saw the strawberries and champagne set out and said, "Oh look, how sweet that is for whoever is going to receive it." She turned to find her fiancé on his knee with a ring in his hand.

Another story involved a girl who used to dance for Royal Caribbean International, and her fiancé setting up his proposal. While on stage, the cruise director said he had a mystery door prize and called her name as the winner. He told the girl to close her eyes and to choose either a bottle of champagne, or the gift behind the curtain.

While her eyes remained shut, her fiancé came forward and bent down on one knee with the ring in his hands. Zack remembers thinking how sensational it was to be a part of that event, and maybe, during a hardship in their lives, that memory might even pop up to smooth over any misunderstandings that young couple may experience later in life.

chapter 12: may I help you?

"We are more fragile so everything that happens is deeper than in a normal environment."

Adrian Theodoru, Guest Services Manager, Romania

Guest Services personnel have a fulfilling challenge, of listening to complaints or compliments. Their attitude suggests that no matter how you see it, people do them a favor by bringing to their attention difficulties while cruising.

Daily challenges give crew members the opportunity to bring happiness. The staff, working with Guest Services, solves problems, and in return receives positive energy from the cruise guest. The financial opportunities of cruise work can exceed those offered in Romania.

Time away from home allows you to make an investment emotionally in the people you share your time with onboard, and your new job turns into your life.

Having financial stability, making new friends, practicing English, meeting people from exotic corners of the world, and traveling to places that represented just locations in an atlas represent some of the benefits that come with the job.

These combine into an opportunity to learn something new. Every guest creates a new scenario, so guiding the guest service staff involves training them to keep an open mind without projecting themselves into the scene.

Mr. Theodoru says, "The challenge of working problems out was what actually convinced me to leave my country. In the long term, whatever we learn here helps on a professional and personal level. That is what I learn from our guests. You are dealing with a new scenario every time, and you need to keep an open mind. You cannot project yourself [to impose on the guests], although you must have access to everything that goes on around you."

Working a few months and then taking a few months off offers a lifestyle that takes some adjustment.

We shed many tears when saying farewell to parents and friends at the airport, but seeing friends back on ship brightens the return. Because of the work environment, crew members learn to enjoy everything that comes their way a million times more, like making new friendships. Back home, while sitting at a bar or working out in a gym, you might choose to ignore those around you.

Ask Adrian about Romanian history

"Whether you're offering a nice gesture or creating a new friendship, everything is more intense because we are separated from family. We are more fragile. So, everything that happens is felt more] deeply than in a normal environment," Mr. Theodoru said.

Romania, an eastern European country, claims a rich history. Consider it a great destination to visit, according to Mr. Theodoru.

What language do they speak in Romania? A tiny country in the center of Eastern Europe, Romania has its own charming language. Distinguishing Romania from any other eastern bloc country is the fact that they speak a Romance language. Isolated and surrounded by Slavic languages, the Romanian language is more Latin than Italian, which is where the Latin language once spoken in Dacia, a province of Rome, originated.

The Latin language survived, although the surrounding countries of Russia, Hungary, and Bulgaria have little to do with Latin.

People on the seaside came under Turkey's influence. The strange geography of the mountains also caused Hungary to influence those people. When advised of Romania's nickname, "the cradle of civilization," the traveler wants to understand her better.

I reviewed some legendary questions from guests. A man asked if the toilets used fresh water or salt water. Another time guests asked if the crew sleeps on board the ship.

The funniest story told repeatedly involved the woman who wanted to know how to use the microwave in her room. Of course, she referred to the safe in the closet.

Someone reported spotting a dog in the hallway one time, and nobody ever figured out the truth of the sighting, or how he got on board.

There are 750,000 registered horse carts in Romania.

The challenges of ship life that crew members experience can feel overwhelming to them, but their comfortable environment helps them cope.

One hundred percent of the crew members who pass along the long corridor that goes from the bow to the stern on deck two, (affectionately called "I-95" by all the employees), will smile.

Projecting yourself as available for every situation that comes along helps you do your best to assist.

Every service you offer contributes to the overall morale of guests as well as staff.

Adjusting to ship life and aligning a realistic approach to working with Royal Caribbean International leads to personal contentment in such a unique environment.

Meeting people from all over the world creates a bond that often results in crew opening their homes to one another.

Invitations to home countries allow intimate relationships to build between crew members who then have a better understanding of that part
of the world.

"With so many nationalities, it's a funny feeling, you know, between: Are you on vacation or are you actually going to work with these people?"

Ivo Jahn, Germany, Executive Chef

In Germany, sixteen-year-old Ivo Jahn started on the pathway toward fulfilling his dream of becoming a chef. Working in Switzerland until nineteen added to his experience. Loving the work gave him the initiative to move back to Germany for a master's degree and then on to Ireland for a summer season to improve his English skills. Adventure called, and with only a flight ticket and three hundred dollars, he moved to New Zealand.

Creates curries from scratch

"It was a great adventure. I fine-tuned my English and did a lot of reading in the dictionary for missed words. After this, unfortunately, the money went a little low because these kinds of jobs are great for experience but not so great for your pocket or your bank account. It's a childhood dream.

Tonight's menu: French onion soup

When I first started becoming a chef, I already had this in mind; *you need to go to a ship one day*. Maybe the basic idea was a little more romantic, something about sailing a ship.

Bubbling tubs: gourmet sauce

While you look at the reality of it, very few people work on a sailing ship. Maybe they have a tiny little galley, with no capacity to build chef skills, and maybe the experience is not so great, working there. I would say, as a European chef, you don't really go in your younger years on a ship. It's more like you gain a little experience, and then you assume a seniority role. The majority of my cooks, they pretty much are not European, but those in management are a good mixture from the Philippines to all over Europe. I had the pleasure of starting as executive sous chef. We do not hire straight executive chefs because there is just too much of a demand. You need to know a little bit about the operation from the bottom before you become the head of the operation," says Ivo.

Assembly line ready for lunch

The ship, *Independence of the Seas*, based in the UK, set the tone for Ivo. He started from scratch, learning the basics from the senior culinary management, a completely different approach than just working as a chef.

When *Oasis of the Seas* became the top project with all new menus and staff for another 1,000 passengers, Ivo assumed more responsibility. Opening *Allure of the Seas* called for moving twenty-five percent of the *Oasis of the Seas* staff over [to the Allure of the Seas], which made his job much easier.

Mixing cake dough

Ivo says, "It was a piece of cake, which may not be the right description, but opening *Allure of the Seas* went smoothly."

Pouring sugar-free frosting

An executive chef's day begins with touring all the food venues open for breakfast, making sure everything is in top form. Answering e-mails, dealing with inventory, and then meetings with all the executive sous chefs over the upcoming days of production follow. Then comes the best part, meeting with the taste panel.

Dinner rolls by the thousands

Discussions arise about what tastes great or what needs improvement. Is the food aesthetically perfect, or do they need to pay more attention to the presentation? Reminders of the past week's issues add to the agenda, for instance, reducing the size of pasta portions.

Rolls ready for table service

Walking the twenty-four food galleys begins again after a lunch break with more e-mails and more tasting before dinner.

Plenty for the cookie jar

Grandma's recipe for cookies

Around 7:30 p.m., the sous chefs come through the main dining areas to check on the meat accounts from the first feeding to see if they need to increase production or make more salads.

Menus change on a daily basis, but the entire week's menu is used week after week, to accommodate the complexity of twenty-four food galleys and all their individual menus.

Corporate chefs in Miami, maintain the quality of food, rewrite the menus, come on board the ship, and implement changes into the system. A chef in a small restaurant might write his own menu or sample his fare to adjust the ingredients order from his vendor.

But on a big ship, any change in the menu might involve using 1,000 pounds more of this or 800 pounds less of that. The test kitchens in Miami look at the offering, and then check the products.

"Every nationality is great to work with. You learn a little more about that country. Let's say Asian people never say no to you. It's a matter of respect.

Then the Caribbean people, just the way they talk, you understand, it's a free style of life.

You see Indian people, they make this gesture to you, and it actually means I am listening to you. At the beginning, you think it makes you crazy or makes you feel crazy, if you communicate in all their ways of communication.

That is one of the things I learned as a manager. I am always amazed over the years because all the HR [Human Resources] issues come to me about the people who have problems with different nationalities.

I never had them. In fact, if you put two Jamaicans in the same cabin, then it's the same issues. I would rather have somebody from a different nationality in my cabin because I think it's nice to know more. I have 350 employees.

Why change the people because you know you have a package, and you know if a person is the way he is and you can accept it, then you know it.

Recognition and approval of individuals is the key. A happy worker is going to be the one that supports you as a chef, meaning employees offer support to those who support them.

Wall of recipes for this week's meals

"If I am doing everything to make their life on the ship great, learn their names, spend even once a month sharing a few words with them, then it's not just like a walk-through.

Personal relationships enhance the work environment. The Filipinos love karaoke, their social event.

When I first heard about it, I was invited, and I came as a courtesy and was finally asked to sing. And I was like, me, sing? They are just going so crazy over this and supporting you to get up and sing.

I came to a point where I really enjoyed this. A few years ago, I was in the Philippines, and I met some of my employees.

I am proud to say we had to do the karaoke. And it was just hilarious, you know, and it's always a win.

We have great vacation experiences here. I'm going to go to Peru as an example.

People offer you their houses even if they won't be home. 'My house is your house,' they say, and 'visit my family.' I think that is a perfect example of what hospitality is to most employees because they would like to share their experiences of their countries," remarks Ivo.

Dessert treats in cool room

The dining staff monitors the production of food with very few leftovers. Sometimes they send the leftovers from a lunch stew or soup to the crew mess hall for dinner. People always love their own local foods.

The Filipinos love their adobo (chicken or pork braised in spices), the Caribbean's their goat curry or jerk chicken (meat dry-rubbed or wet-marinated with a very hot spice mixture and roasted over aromatic charcoal), and Indians their curry-flavored dishes. Because of all the new and different dishes, Ivo uses real spices to make curry sauces.

He says, "I know in Germany there are people who make a curry sauce or something, but we should not even call it a curry sauce, because they use curry powder or something basic. But cooking with the right spices from scratch, well, that is an experience. I really like the food the main nationalities are bringing on."

Vacations equal seeing the world for Ivo. He feels that having the ability to click off [turn off cruise work] after four months of work helps him enjoy the two-month free period. On his next vacation, he plans to climb Mt. Kilimanjaro, but then that only takes two weeks. A big motorbike tour to France for a little wine and friends in Bulgaria will fill the time on the way back. To maintain balance, he makes consistent trips to the gym. He sees himself as a world traveler and offers this advice in the form of a question: what job in the world offers you four months of paid vacation per year?

Germany: Employees get 20-30 days of paid vacation per year.

Ivo says, "I would rather have people say, 'You look pretty skinny for a chef." I see it as a compliment, because I do try to maintain a good body, which is not so easy, especially when you are around good food all day. But you don't need to eat a lot to taste. Rather, to taste the sauce, you need half a teaspoon. The bad part is that a lot of things are really great and you feel like you could eat a little bit more of those things."

Daren, a sous chef, offers a tour of the kitchen facilities so passengers get an inside look at how a dining room prepares food for thousands of guests at every meal.

A sous chef assists the executive chef, a sort of middle management. His duties include the following: food preparation, production, supervising personnel, checking inventory, supplies, safety, sanitation issues, and ensuring maintenance of quality and cost standards.

The largest dining room in the world on the Allure of the Seas ship consists of three levels, with deck five reserved for those wanting to dine without reservations. Decks three and four seat more than 4,000 people in one evening.

The pantry section prepares all the cold salads, and soups like gazpacho. During a typical night, 400-600 salads wait in huge refrigerators for waiters to serve. Six or seven expensive ovens, the most modern and efficient made, are installed on each deck and have the ability to bake with convection, as regular ovens, using dry steam, or any combination of those options. These ovens reduce food waste, while meats cook at 160 degrees for eleven hours, keeping the moisture in.

The bakery boasts a machine that makes 4000 rolls in one hour. The walk-in refrigerators smell like groves of fruit trees when ripe and ready for picking. The cakes, torts, and mousses fill racks to the ceiling.

Allure of the Seas spends close to a half-million dollars a week on food. Daren came from the British Army, having worked as a chef feeding thousands in Afghanistan and Iraq.

His first cruise and first ship? *Allure of the Seas*.

Edible art

Another crew member confirmed Ivo's point about a dedicated crew. While serving coffee, she told about how much she loved working for Royal Caribbean International and how she wouldn't trade her job for anything.

When asked about the food for the crew she said with a smile, "I'm not lying. Every day there is good food, and someone else cleans up and washes the dishes."

What did she miss the most while on board working?

She smiles with, "My family. They are my heart and soul. I don't know how people cannot love their children. My son died in a car accident at the age of twenty-one. He died on Friday, and we buried him on Sunday. If I would have been home, I could have been with him a few more days before he left us.

By the time I got home from the ship, he was gone. When guests start talking about their children or ask about mine, I have to walk away or I would start to cry."

With ice cream on the side, please

What is it about food on cruise ships? You plan for it ("where we will go the first night for dinner?"), you anticipate each meal (let's try the seafood buffet for lunch today), and you reminisce when you return home (remember that waiter who talked us into second helpings of lobster?)

Dramatic changes have come about in cruise-ship cuisine including breath-taking new dining rooms, exotic foods on menus, and options galore from specialty restaurants, little snack bars, roving waiters with trays of canapés, midnight desert buffets, and twenty-four-hour room service.

Healthy gourmet includes sugar-free items and menus offering low calorie delights. It's no wonder that cruise passengers everywhere are saying, "bon appetite."

chapter 14: self-described vampires

"So, we are vampires. We stay away from the sunlight and work during the night."

JJ Macdonald, Casino Hostess, UK

The London Standard newspaper's classifieds advertised, "Would you like to work great hours and become a glamorous croupier or casino dealer, work nine to five (nights) and become a vampire?"

From age four, JJ Macdonald's dreams while ice dancing in England turned to Olympic gold medals. When it came time to earn real money, three options played in her head. Join the Metropolitan police force, train as a medical examiner with Westminster College, or become a croupier. Fate would decide. The first recruitment drive in the London paper set her course of life. London Clubs came out with the croupier ad two weeks later, and they selected her name out of the 6,000 applications. After two cruises with friends, she decided if they treated their passengers this well, then they must treat their crew the same, and so she decided to take the job.

JJ describes her typical day as casino hostess as flat-out crazy. JJ considers her work like that of a help desk, answering questions from, "How do I make a long-distance call from my room?" to "Can I see my room bill if I put my card in the slot machine?" In fact, JJ has received many off-the-wall questions, such as, "Will the points give me back all the cash that I lost during the cruise?" "I just lost $80 in one of your slot machines; how can I get it back?" "I am lost; will the slot machine tell me how to get to my stateroom?" "What's my room number?" "From which slot machine can I buy cigarettes?" "How much money do I need to lose to get a Taylor Swift concert ticket?"

JJ tells the story of the man with early Alzheimer's or pre-dementia who came to her desk every night at 8:00 and asked what room he was in. From Day 1 through Day 7, she would write down his room number, name, and how to get from A to B. Every night he would come back again, and JJ would hand him the information with, "There you go, my love." They say that goldfish have a second memory, and they just go around the tank again, seeing everything for the first time. Are we so different?

Ice dancer, turned casino hostess

Another story involved a mother who wanted to enter her eleven-year-old son in the Taylor Swift look-alike concert competition in order to win tickets. She bought wigs, makeup, and had expensive costumes made. When it came time for the competition, her son ranked second place. The mother was devastated and complained that she spent all this time and money and therefore should have won the prize tickets. To console her, Royal Caribbean International ended up giving her concert tickets anyway.

Casino workers treat millionaires exactly the same way they treated the gentleman who came into JJ's London casino with string holding up his brown stained pants, spending his weekly 200 pounds of wages on roulette and returning the next Friday to lose another paycheck.

When asked what motivated her to do her best work, she answered, "Helping people. One of my biggest drives is that I care about human beings, which is why I wanted to join the police force. If I can help somebody in any way, regardless of how small or insignificant the act is, if there is anything I can do to remedy their issues, I will. A casino host position means you have to fly by the seat of your pants and make fast decisions. It's almost like being a master chess player where you have four or five moves. In case the scenario of A, B or C doesn't work, then you have the offshoot of the next scenario, depending on what the player decides or what the next words are out of the player's mouth. You need to have another set of solutions ready, branching off from that. The longer you are in this position, the more situations and experiences you see, the more resolutions you have in your arsenal to remedy a particular situation. You put those remedies in a vault and store them until the next time the need comes up. Going above and beyond: it's part of Royal Caribbean International's credo. It's our mantra," JJ states.

One of the crew members on board who previously worked as a detective flattered JJ by saying how good she would have been in forensics or police enforcement.

The escalators in the London Tube equal two round-the-world trips every week.

"Is there stress?" I ask.

"I have seen people completely lose the plot, the reason for being in the casino. Absolutely, because you have so many variances in gambling, so many factors involved, which push every single solitary psychological button the gamblers can possibly think of. The fact that the customers have lost money, have had too much to drink, or argued with a spouse about too much time in the casino, all lead to one little thing being out of place and it's like a rocket bottle. Just because somebody is puffed in the face shouting and screaming doesn't mean my life is at risk. It just means that I have to help them.

"So as a casino host," JJ says, "it is my job to help those players, whether it's this or that or something more serious like let's take a time out, like a situation if we were home on a Sunday afternoon. Sit on the deck, take a deep breath and relax. If somebody would make a reality TV show about a casino, the ratings would be unbelievable, just because of what happens with the general interaction between guests and their reactions to the games. It's hilarious, absolutely hilarious."

Regarding the cultural diversity of the crew members and the guests, JJ commented on issues that could arise over politics, sports, or religion. She said that focusing on the job and encouraging teamwork, help alleviate interpersonal conflict with every new encounter. Politics and religion become a moot point and never an issue. She can talk sports with guests. The football teams range from Manchester United, Liverpool, Arsenal, Everton, to any number of teams from all over the world. Catholic, Baptist, Jewish, Muslim, all create a cornucopia of religions. Royal Caribbean International allows every culture to celebrate their religions and mark their country's holidays as they wish, like Canada Day for the Canadians and Independence Day on July 4th for the Americans. Whether a person comes from a poor part of India or a wealthy area of London, the ship treats everybody as an equal.

"Casino work is almost addictive," says JJ. "Once a person is in the industry, it is extraordinarily hard to get out because of the lifestyle, the money we earn, and the opportunities that are given to us. I've been all over the world and I've never had to pay for it. I've visited places my parents and grandparents only dream of going or haven't even heard of. People in my line of work rise to a level of lifestyle that we couldn't possibly have in any other job, unless we were in our own business and had the freedom to go to the Maldives on a whim for two weeks, or to South Africa for three weeks. Oh, we are vampires! There will be weeks that go by where we choose not to get off on a port day, unless we want to sacrifice some sleep and get some fresh air and sunshine. We'll be awake from dusk till dawn so we won't see daylight. Sleep is a huge topic of discussion."

When asked if she lives in her own little world, socializing and sticking together with colleagues, she responded in the affirmative.

"We do, we do. And that gets wild because that is also a release as well. Shopping. All the girls get together and do retail therapy. We just had a casino party that started around 3:30 a.m. and went until about 7:00 a.m. That is our time to have a party and so we are vampires. We stay away from the sunlight and work during the night. I know that every casino family on board every ship is extremely tight, probably tighter than any other department on board, basically because we have long hours, and we all look after each other."

Homesickness only brings to mind one thing for JJ and her husband, Ian Macdonald, whom she met on her first contract with Royal Caribbean International. They both put their hearts into their work while on board the ship. They both love to cook and miss spending hours with recipe books, trying to decide what to have for dinner before heading to the market for fresh fish or vegetables while off the ship. To keep from falling asleep at four in the afternoon, a little self-discipline means staying awake those first twenty-four hours until they are tired enough to fall asleep at ten in the evening. JJ considers the ice rink as off limits. After training for the Olympics, she knows seeing the ice shows and getting back on the rink might start an addiction she couldn't work in to her schedule.

"There are thousands of books out there on the strategies of throwing dice, even slot machines," JJ warns. "We will tip people off and say, just play on your luck. I think a lot of people just play on instinct, and a lot play on intuition. I always rely on mine. A long time ago I didn't. Then I reached thirty (years of age). I need to listen to that little voice in my head that says, 'Take a left, JJ, instead of a right.'"

Casinos are a wonderful place to resist the urge to over analyze every choice. Intuition. The sixth sense. Our internal compass. Basically, with intuition your brain is on autopilot.

As Alan Alda said, "You have to leave the city of your comfort and go into the wilderness of your intuition."

Casinos offer one of the biggest sources of recreation and entertainment on the cruise ship. Whether intuition is called to action or gambling is used simply as a stress buster or for personal enjoyment, it acts to produce a thrilling experience

chapter 15: ship shape

"Maybe once or twice a week, I have a chance to call them up and say, oh I miss you, and then they sing a song for me...and I...just cry tears of joy."

Joseph Capiral, Facilities Cleaning Manager, Philippines

Although Joseph's physical therapy degree in the Philippines qualified him for his gym instructor position, he felt he had different avenues to explore. He looks back on advice from friends telling him to practice his profession, but he feels blessed with his choice now. Working two or three contracts as a FCM (facilities cleaning manager) and then back to more education, he explains, has been his career path. Compared to the instructor job, working on a cruise ship offers rewards, like helping a sister finish her studies, and embracing the dream of travel by going to places unimaginable.

After a short adjustment period to his new environment of sea life and meeting people from all corners of the world, Joseph moved from *Nordic Empress*, the smallest of the Royal Caribbean International fleet, to *Radiance of the Seas*, where his father worked as a purser in charge of accounts and paperwork.

Filipinos send more text messages than the US and Europe combined: 400 million daily.

"I couldn't even imagine I would be working alongside my dad. Everybody was asking me, 'Are you brothers?' because we didn't really look exactly alike, and I said, 'If he were my brother, then he is the older one, not me.'

"I would say it is very rewarding working on a ship but hard to be away from my family, especially my sister, who at that time I was attached to. The first time I called home after getting my first job on a ship, I didn't cry even when I talked with my parents. I cried when I talked with my sister. And all of them in the room said, 'Are you okay?' I am okay, it's just that...these are happy tears, not that I'm crying for something, I am just happy. My sister was encouraging me with, 'You can survive.' She was really my inspiration. I'd say encouraging her is one of my accomplishments. Yeah, even my grandparent was telling me, 'You really help your family, both inside and out.' They were dreaming that I would be working in a hospital. But my career happened to turn from the right to the left," Joseph admits.

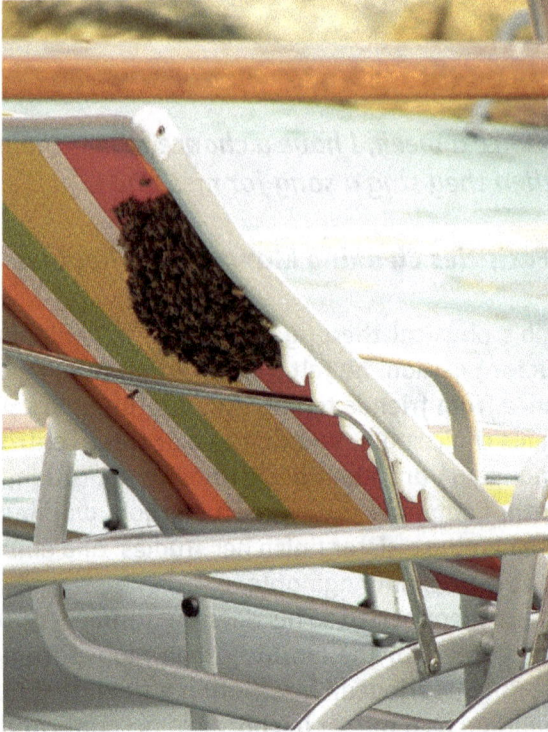

Bee swarm on the pool deck: rare emergency

Allure of the Seas has three facilities cleaning managers: one takes care of the interior, one the open decks, and one supervises the night cleaning. Joseph works the open decks, including the only salt-water pool on board, with its beach umbrellas, daily sunshine, and opportunities to meet and help guests. He started as a pool attendant and within several months worked his way up to assistant.

He tells his team: "There are a lot of avenues right now, and I was proud of myself and my accomplishments, and the company really helped me manage my career. It's really inspiring. You can see how patience and hard work really paid off. That's the only reward we need. I started where you guys started. Treat everybody equally. If you think that because I am from the Philippines, I will give favors only to Filipinos instead of you, no. I am straightforward and I listen to both sides.

"I have thirty-five under my umbrella. I have twenty-six new hires. I helped my guys to move one step higher, and I just have to suffer the consequences at the beginning, working with inexperienced employees, but I will say… basically all these trainings are hard work and take perseverance when it comes to teaching these guys what to do."

Experts arrive to vacuum the bees

Eventually, those twenty-six new hires jell together, building relationships, spending time together after work and surprising Joseph with, "Chief, how are you doing?"

"Work is work, and pleasure is pleasure. You can talk to me at any time. I can be flexible. We are all enjoying ourselves. We don't want to be left in the four corners of the room and then not asking for help," Joseph says.

Breaking the language barrier plays a huge role in effective communication. The Filipinos study English from kindergarten through high school.

Some of the new hires from China learned English only in high school, and having never practiced or polished the language, they have a difficult time onboard. The Rosetta Stone language learning journey is available on the ship. Managers encourage crew to use and practice English every day.

"I told my guys, from humble beginnings I started" Joseph says. "Hopefully [they] happen to get something special from my stories.

Perseverance, hard work, and patience are virtues that were given to me. They were telling me of the leadership capabilities that I have and that I am a strong motivator to my guys. I will keep on reaching out to my guys. It's not every day that I have to tell them they might be getting up on the wrong side of the bed. In appreciation, since you get the good guest comments, I could give you a shore excursion tour or credit in one of these special restaurants. That is one of my ways of rewarding them.

When we've had a tough week, I will say to the guys, "Maybe you can take time to go outside and relax and refresh your mind, and I know you don't want to see the ship for the meantime so just enjoy yourself. "That is really motivating for them," says Joseph.

Living in a small cabin with a stranger who isn't sensitive to your cultural background stirs the emotions. Quickly cabin mates learn flexibility. With new adjustments comes new knowledge about another culture and its customs.

Sometimes, even between people from the same country, personalities just don't mesh, and talks with managers help resolve such issues.

Royal Caribbean International does its best to honor request forms for change of roommates.

A benefit for Filipinos comes from one of their government agencies setting up a savings account with the ship, sending back a certain percentage of his salary to wherever the crew member designates, either into a savings account, to a spouse, or both. That way, when on vacation back home in the Philippines, they have something to access without the need to worry about exchange rates.

When questioned what might surprise a foreigner about the Philippines, Joseph answered with, "Filipinos are really good at hospitality. I mean, we will find ways...to make you comfortable."

Filipinos make up twenty-five percent of the crew onboard *Allure of the Seas*. Of 2,186 people, 511 are from the Philippines. The engine room employs the largest percentage, as Filipinos have a reputation for being creative with their minds.

If a part is broken, they figure out a way to recycle and fix it instead of relying on something new. It's almost as if they wake up in the morning with new ideas.

Joseph and Gelashe: mission accomplished

The training the men go through before working for a ship is very specific. From high school, an individual takes a basic safety training class called SOLAS or the International Convention for Safety of Life at Sea. Individuals who wish to pursue a career in seafaring should complete the Basic Safety Course (BSC) training. This is a prerequisite for applying for a Seaman's Book and getting a Certificate of Completion. Training includes firefighting and survival techniques. Applicants must be high school graduates, at least eighteen years old, and speak, read, and write English to complete the list of requirements.

The foundation of a Filipino's life centers on family principles. They are highly motivated to do side jobs to earn extra money to send back home.

Joseph says, "My family and my son really motivate me to work hard. At one point, I am talking with my one-year-old son, but I am talking with tears, and I know that he feels it, and he just cannot say it, but he shows it with his expression. So, it somehow put a soft spot in my heart so I would want to be with my employees all day long to do and make these sacrifices. Even for my partner, it is hard to be away, fifteen thousand miles and twelve hours' time difference. My self-esteem, motivation, and determination have developed me as a person. I have been offered an abundance of knowledge. It's really rewarding. There is no such thing as an easy job.

❦ chapter 16: let's float a resort

"With understanding comes tolerance and acceptance for the guest care team."

Raimund Gschaider, Hotel Director, Austria

The screening process selects new hires based on their skills in hospitality. Crew expects to offer services in hopes that the guests will return. As opposed to land jobs, the social and professional aspects of living exist together. Concentrating on the job, leaving religion and politics at home, acts like a key for folks from Croatia and Serbia or Pakistan and India to get along.

Advice to the young: explore the world

Mr. Gschaider, hotel director, embarked on his career from Austria with the idea of seeing the world. Twenty-eight years later, he has earned four stripes on his uniform and still has the goal to make the guests' experience the best. Of the 2,170 crew, he supervises over 2,000 and takes responsibility for the fiscal integrity or profit as well. With growth in size and complexity of the cruise ship, the responsibilities increase. Onboard the ship, he coordinates, supervises, directs and manages all services that the guests experience like entertainment, food, and beverage programs, cruise programs, housekeeping, guest services, retail, casino, human relations, and the IT functions. Mr. Gschaider says, "It's pretty much everything other than driving the ship and operating the nautical side. I make sure everybody communicates well and coordinates. There is the safety side and the human resources side. With 2,170 employees, that element takes a lot of attention and focus. As the ships have grown in size, more so in complexity, the various responsibilities have added up, and that brings my position more to directing the experience rather than being part of the experience. The secret to operating a ship this size is, you have to create an organizational structure and put the right people in the right place to make it work. Clearly, we have outgrown the possibility for any one person or any one group of people to successfully operate such a ship. We tend to hire people who want to be part of the hospitality industry. We are in a business where you provide great service to people and make them feel comfortable. I think anybody who doesn't like people should not go into this kind of professional environment. I think they should repair cars or do something else more suitable. "There is no high pressure here. It is a lifestyle. What really separates ships and jobs on land is that here your job and your life are interconnected. Not your life as a whole, but your day-to-day life. Whereas on land you finish your job and go home. Here you finish your job and spend it in the same area on the same ship, and you meet with the same people you work with. Obviously, your private life is governed by some rules and regulations. People are focused on why they are here: for the most part, to earn money and provide a living for themselves. It's a very fair and transpiring, also developing, environment. Opportunities are available to anybody to have a great future, because the company is growing very success-fully. Crew can have fun at times, and of course, on rare occasions, practical jokers become creative. Imagine the embarrassment, years ago, when someone put the captain's car on the heliport, the wind increased, and the crane needed to move it back was not in operation. "A lot of regulations and compliance as-pects have changed with time and technology. In the old days, some twenty years ago, life offered more freedom and simplicity on ships. At one time, folks put on insulated suits in Alaska, jumped in the fjords [narrow inlets] and climbed icebergs to chip ice for a drink. Glacier ice over 1,000 years old created a base for ice sculptures on board. Safety regulations prevent swimming off a ship in today's world, and with environmentalists protecting our glaciers, our ice sculptures come from man-made ice."

Over 60% of Austria's electricity comes from renewable sources.

"I was on a ship for the first time, and we went to the Far East, which took us through the Panama Canal across to Europe, through the Suez Canal, down to India and up around Thailand and Malaysia. We ended up in Singapore for dry dock. We took the guests on a forty-two-day round trip from Hong Kong up the Chinese coast toward Japan. It happened to be the same year that there were problems with Taiwan, and because of the tension, the majority of our guests cancelled, and we had to move with fifty percent occupancy. What sticks in my mind? It took us five days to load the ship. China didn't have much to offer [supplies]. In Korea, we only had one shot at gathering everything we needed for the remainder of the trip. Japan was price prohibitive and didn't re-ally fit into our operations," says Mr. Gschaider.

"Russia in those years offered no free market or shopping. Some crew mem-bers found themselves in very challenging situations with the locals and offered cartons of cigarettes for trade (Russian watches were traded for cigarettes).

Curious, I asked, "What other changes have you noticed on board ships?"

"When the boat leaves Port Everglades, life picks up on board. People have medical emergencies, and people unfortunately do at times pass away. Don't forget, a lot of people want to experience a particular cruise or see a certain destination in their time, and sometimes people have to struggle to participate. With an increase in ship size, the former reliance on people stepping forward in emergencies has changed, replaced with trained care teams, including three doctors, five nurses and a secretary. Their response time after a 911 phone call takes about ninety seconds on *Allure of the Seas*."

People wonder what staff misses about home while on the ship. But after spending twenty-eight years living the ship life, Mr. Gschaider responded to a question about what he misses about ship life when home: "Here in a world where everything is important, you go back home and listen to a discussion about little nitty things. Things at home seem narrower and more predictable. Upsets over minor issues become a common affair. People complain they had to add an hour to their forty-hour workweek, while on a ship you do whatever it takes with a smile. Oh, my heart goes out to them. I don't worry about how many hours I work. I worry about getting the job done and taking care of every detail. So, my heart changed here with this job. It doesn't matter where my colleagues come from, especially those who are in this lifestyle for a while. We all agreed that we'd become world-wise, and we are far more open-minded than other people who have never left home.

"People are here for a couple of purposes. Some want to see the world when they are young, but then when they are here for more than two years, they customize the idea because of the income and security, seeing a career opportunity. I am Austrian and there are young people at home who don't have a job they want, and I am trying to tell them, why don't you go out in the world? I mean, you have education. Say to yourself I am going to do something else for a few years. There is, I don't know, a hesitation or reluctance because they hear different sides, like the income is not good, or I don't want to leave my family, or I don't want to stay here so long. I think in today's world in many cultures, especially the economically successful cultures, I am talking Central Europe and Northern America where the economies and the social nets are strong, people are less inclined to be adventurous and take opportunities.

"Our employee base does shift from time to time from certain nationality groups. When the eastern bloc countries opened up in the nineties, we got a lot of Romanians and Bulgarian crew members. Because they are now, for five to ten years, a part of this organization, you find them in very advanced management opportunities. So you see that growth and that advancement in a very short period of time. When I started, we had quite a lot of Norwegians on the nautical side and a lot of German-speaking people in food and beverage. You find very few Norwegians in today's world of cruising. I may have said I am a spy and try to talk people at home into doing this," Mr. Gschaider says with a twinkle in his eye. "Officers reinforce the foundations in their training examples. The support from the upper levels ripples through the crew. For example, the ship sailed for five to six weeks before any paying passenger came on to get the crew familiar with all the new facilities, stations, and rules. The training emphasized the international flavor of things, the blending of the many cultures represented. The people remain the same, and their opinions remain the same, but they learn to get along with a larger mission in mind. "Nothing is based on nationalities or gender. It's simply that you have your position, and the way you lean politically or religiously is a private matter, and there is no criterion no point of comparison here on board the ship. We don't deal very often with global issues. You need to keep this diversity. The moment you let one nationality become too big and too powerful, it usually causes distrust. For example, if you have a dining room and eighty percent of the headwaiters are from nationality X, then the other thirty nationalities in the dining room will become suspicious, and they may not think they are getting the right opportunities. This ship goes to Jamaica, and naturally, it attracts more Caribbean crew members since they are closer to home, and it gives them the opportunity to say hello to the family. Is this a good thing? Well, it's a good thing for the Jamaicans, but at the same time we have 1,800 other crew members who don't have that opportunity to come home every two weeks. We have to keep it balanced.

"Some cultures struggle with the basics, like eye contact. In the older Caribbean generations, parents warned children to avoid looking someone in the eye. You [the crew staff] know that is not polite to do that, and you expect the management to say, 'Hey, look at me when I talk to you.' It's for us to know what we are dealing with. It's one thing for us to expect the employees to change. But for you, as the management or the leader who is entrusted with operating and understanding people, knowing where people come from and reactions from certain personalities, it's for us to understand them first," says Mr. Gschaider.

His advice to the United Nations, "Send their folks to a place like this, where the task and team are important, and the young folks [working as staff on board] will return home better than before, be more tolerant, and be able to work in a more diverse and dynamic environment. "There is more satisfaction here than working with self-defined standards." Each day for Mr. Gschaider offers different issues to deal with attentive service without being intrusive. He encourages the idea of the guests having the holiday of their life-time.

chapter 17: work with, and become, a kid

"It's a sheltered life, with so much mothering."

Holly Boulind, Cruise-Director Staff, South Africa

While working as an actress, Holly, born in South Africa, met a lady who suggested she apply for a cruise ship job. Her original idea was to work for one contract, which turned into two, and now she loves working as a staff member for the Cruise Director.

In charge of fun

Holly works all over the ship in various jobs, including helping host parties and giving craft and art classes.

"The big advantage is making friends with so many different nationalities, and you can travel on vacation time. My friend Flo and I went to Argentina on vacation. One person from our team is from Australia so we have accommodations there and plan to visit in January."

When asked what she missed about ship life when on vacation, she answered with, "I miss my friends and the social life. We are really, really looked after. It's a sheltered life, with so much mothering. For six months, your team becomes your family, so when one member leaves, or you go home, you really miss each other. We all get homesick, because we are not home for Christmas, so our team does a Secret Santa. We draw up a list of things we want for Christmas and share it with the team.

"Our hours are never nine to five. We take naps so we can focus on our work sessions."

Crew friends

The best food she has tasted since leaving home? She is a vegetarian and ravioli is the best!

Working with different cultures gives you a new perspective on the world. You become more open-minded, see how people respond and suddenly realize people are so different, like Holly's friend Flo from Argentina, who eats dinner late. Holly, who lived in Britain most of her life typically ate dinner 9:00 p.m. Now she eats dinner at 6:00 p.m.

When she goes back home, friends ask what she doesn't like about her job. "Line dancing," she says.

Everyone has a hero. Holly's is her mother. She stated she would like to be one-tenth to others of what her mom is to her.

Crafts: Nigeria and Philly meet on board

When asked about the one thing she has done that she is most proud of, she did not hesitate in her response:

"Coming to cruise ships," she answers. "There is no one here to disappoint you. It's the most adventurous decision to make, to be on your own, so far from home. Even if you want to leave, you are on your own, making decisions alone."

When the arts and crafts workshop begins on the first day of a cruise, everyone is a stranger. Working with different guests who might speak only Spanish is a challenge. One guest asked if the elevator took him to the back of the ship. Another asked what time the midnight buffet was.

South Africa generates two-thirds of Africa's electricity.

"Mostly it is women who sign up for the arts and crafts workshops, and they begin telling stories about their families. By the end of the cruise, everyone is best friends, and you think it is sad that the week is over and begin to wonder if next week's guests will be as warm and friendly and fun," Holly says.

Strangers build friendships with crafts

Holly shares all the qualities of a great friend when first introduced. With that British accent, she addresses you with, "Nice to meet you, love." Vibrant and full of energy, she captures the heart of every guest she meets. With her smile alone, she could talk a seventy-year-old into coming to a midnight party. The ship is full of people like Holly, who share a little piece of their culture just by saying, "Hello."

Bracelets: a path to friendship

chapter 18: sing, dance, serve

"Now when I go home, I want to go back to work."

Tamra Barnett, Beverage Department, Jamaica

"Once the music is playing and it's good, I'm dancing and singing and doing everything 'cause I'm Jamaican, and we tend to love music. You either have it or you don't," Tamra Barnett, a bar server on the ship, says proudly, "I have been dancing since I was a kid in Jamaica, and I have been singing since I can't remember. My mom says when she picked me up from school, people would turn around and look at me 'cause I was so small, but yet I knew all the words to the song. And momma would say, 'She know her book work just the same.'"

Once shy: now enthusiastic singing server

Three and a half years ago, Tamra's first contract began with tears and thoughts of "I want to go home." Quickly, everything started to fall into place, including exposure to new foods. Besides missing family, she has to think hard when asked what she misses about home. She finally decided that going to bed at eight o'clock would seem appealing.

"Trust me," she says, "you really miss everything [about the ship when you go home again]." You miss all the parties. The islands. Working at home, you could never afford to take a vacation like this. And the fact that you are here, it's like a vacation that you are getting paid to have, because you get to see all these beautiful islands. My experiences have been wide because I was sent to Europe and got to see that part of the world. I was in Paris, Gibraltar, and Madeira, Portugal. They are so beautiful, and at home, there is not much to see as you are just in that little box. But here you are exposed to everything, and you get experience. So it's good, really good!"

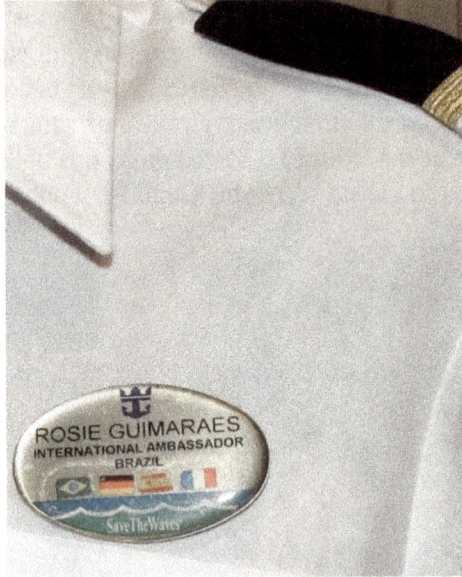

Language help on board

Tamra followed her father's example for cruise ship work. Her sister, jealous for years of Tamra's adventures, found her new job on the Norwegian Jewel rewarding, especially after meeting a man who used to work with her father and has shared some wonderful stories about him. Both sisters take pride in helping their families and friends with so much more because they are earning more money to share than when they worked at home.

"Strangers? I don't consider guests to be strangers. They are long lost friends. They tell themselves, okay, we are going to meet some people. We are going to interact, to get to know them, know a little bit about their background, and I tell myself the same thing about them. That is why I am in this job. I am a people person. And it interests me when I can learn something about your culture, different things that you do in your country and how different it is in my country," Tamra says.

While taking a business course with a girl from Trinidad, Tamra learned a lot about that country, so she felt comfortable with her first ship roommate, a Trinidadian. Her second roommate, a girl from India, taught her so much about the Indian culture, including things like abandonment by one's family if one gets pregnant before marriage. An island like Jamaica offers little opportunity for meeting people from the far corners of the world, like Romania or Bulgaria, not to mention learning about their food, customs, and languages.

Ask about his North African heritage

A bar server's world means mingling with guests and hearing all types of stories. Some make you smile, like one time someone asked Tamra, "The rising tide, does it go up or does it go down?" Her boss explained the desirable attitude of treating no questions as silly and of trying to answer all questions. Guests face a new environment, especially on the first day.

Frustration with accents faces all crew members who work with the guests. Your contact with dozens of nationalities, both during work and while relaxing or sharing meals, helps you deal with the guests. Tamra says her advice is to slow down and listen. Some people learn quicker than others do, but you learn from each other.

Tamra, when commenting on working with somebody new, said you might wonder where might this person come from, maybe a country you have never heard of before. Maybe you learn new drinks or new ways to finish your work.

Once she showed someone a new way to walk to work, taking advantage of a shortcut. Often to new hires, Tamra says, "Come, I'll take you under my wing. I'll teach you what I know and you teach me what you know."

One night a guest came into the Diamond Lounge and said, "Tamra," and she answered, "Yes, what did I do now?"

He asked, "What are you doing here? I left you on *Oasis*?"

She replied, "Yes, but they kicked me off *Oasis* and sent me here to *Allure of the Seas*."

Jamaica: Only two countries earned more Miss World contests.

The guest requested a Sex on the Beach drink, not available, as the Diamond Lounge has a set menu. Tamra worked her magic, remembering the non-liquor-based morning mixes offered a wide variety of flavors, including peach. The Sex on the Beach drink requires Peach Schnapps, Vodka, cranberry juice, and orange juice, so the only thing missing from the lounge was the Peach Schnapps. Substituting the peach morning mix to complete the drink surprised and pleased the guest so much, he returned every night for more.

Another guest, a foreign ambassador, asked for Makers Mark bourbon, which the lounge didn't carry. Tamra promised she would find some for the next day. When the ambassador returned, another server couldn't help him. Tamra arrived from her break and saved the day, within minutes offering a Makers Mark Manhattan.

The guest told her boss, "I don't know what she is doing but she needs to keep it up. Not one day I pass by here and she isn't singing and dancing and always happy."

Does an island without snow and chimneys still celebrate Santa and all the festive gatherings of family and entertainment associated with the traditional white Christmas? Jamaicans celebrate not only Santa Claus and Silent Night (even a reggae version) but also Jonkanoo or John Canoe, a special island tradition. Men parade through the streets in costumes of wild Indians, devils, and policemen. They even carry small boxes painted like houses on top of their heads.

Today this celebration of loud bands and gigantic costumes appears more for special parties or in rural areas of Jamaica. Grand Markets full of vendors selling firecrackers, candy, pinda, or peanuts, and small toys enliven the town plazas on Christmas Eve. Special hats (which everyone purchases upon entering the market), paper bells, and crepe streamers hang from trees and the sides of buildings. The celebration lasts all day and night and includes church attendance, gift exchanging, and, of course, the feast, which ends with Jamaican-style

Christmas cake made of fruit soaked in rum.

JAMAICAN CHRISTMAS CAKE
6 ounces or 1.5 cups flour
8 ounces butter or margarine
8 ounces sugar
4 eggs
1 pound raisins
1 teaspoon cinnamon
4 ounces mixed fruit peel
4 ounces cherries
8 ounces chopped prunes
Half teaspoon salt
1 cup brandy or wine
1 teaspoon baking powder
1 teaspoon vanilla
2 tablespoons of browning or caramelized sugar

Cream the butter, white sugar, and browning sugar until soft and fluffy. Sift the dry ingredients together. Beat the eggs and wine or brandy together and add to the creamed butter and sugar. Add fruits and then fold in the flour mixture. Do not over beat while mixing. Bake at 350°F for 1.5 hours. Makes one nine-inch round cake.

Tamra recalls a very special Christmas Eve when she misplaced her family. She found a police station and told them she lived over in that neighborhood, pointing to the back of the police station. She told them she knew Mr. Jackson, a policeman friend of the family. A lady happened to walk in the door, recognizing Tamra. When asked if she knew of any family friends, she mentioned Mr. Jackson, so they let the woman take Tamra home to her hysterical mother. Tamra, only eight at the time, remembers saying to her mother, "Mom, are you going to lose me next year?" She loved adventure, always following in her brother's footsteps, whether it be climbing a tree or sneaking off to the beach. After that experience, her mother kept close tabs on her daughter, never allowing her to leave home alone.

Royal Caribbean International offers a wonderful package deal for couples like Tamra and her husband. They met in passing in 2005, before they'd worked on a cruise ship. They worked opposite shifts, so they barely spoke, even though he managed her department. *Independence of the Seas* brought them together, and they shared a drink or two in the crew lounge after work. From friendship to romance, their relationship ended in marriage on the *Oasis* in St. Thomas. By filling out a couples' form, Royal Caribbean International gives couples the opportunity to keep working together and sharing vacation time together.

With a huge smile and a little dance step to her walk, Tamra says, "Once you keep us happy, then we keep the guests happy. It works both ways!"

Sounds like a winning formula!

PART II:

Introduction: the resort floats!

Through the eyes of crew members, you have observed, in Part I, the magic of creating a smooth working team from some seventy-nine countries.

Each cruise ship will have a different manifest listing for crew nations, but you can generalize from this example to any ship in the fleet.

You caught a glimpse of the challenges surrounding each crew member's assignment and how teamwork helped to create that exceptional vacation experience for each guest.

The following pages again peek behind the scenes to complete the picture.

A cruise line is part of a large services industry, dealing with people seeking pleasure. As such, it is a business.

Merely creating an agreeable environment for crew members and avoiding conflict based on ethnic histories would amount to an empty exercise if not linked to the very reason for the existence of this enterprise.

You can easily feel the difference between this business and that of the bits and pieces of the hospitality industry served by planes, trains, rental cars, hotels, restaurants, spas, casinos and sport complexes.

A land-based "resort" combines many of the functions just listed. A cruise ship combines the functions of the fixed-based resort with the functions of the transportation industry as it moves guests from country to country, keeping them rested, entertained, exercised, primped, and fed.

So, the additional interviews below will look at the business side as well as the cultural integration side, since every guest has practical questions beyond the simple curiosity about how "all hands work together."

Of the roughly 2,200 crew members on board the Allure of the Seas, each member has an assignment geared to creating a happy experience for guests, and both the marine and hotel sides of the operation contribute to guest satisfaction. The fact that this company has blended crew from many countries only makes the accomplishment that much more amazing.

chapter 19: who created this floating resort?

"From its very beginning, this company has always been guided by the principles of 'Why Not?'"

While this book was written without interviewing Richard D. Fain Chairman/Chief Executive Officer, Royal Caribbean Cruises Ltd. and Adam M. Goldstein President/CEO, Royal Caribbean International, we saw their fingerprints in the wonderful attitudes of the crew, and their commitment to excellence in serving guests. The leaders' blogs and industry reports about their philosophy underscore their strong principles about doing business.

One could not interview a crew member of Royal Caribbean International without feeling the presence inside the room of the two leaders who created the magic. Their mission of pleasing the guest in such a fashion that the guest will return embeds itself in each member of the team, from the veterans to the newest members. Whether you have experienced such a cruise or are thinking about it, the interviews, telling the crew side of the story, should whet your appetite to forget the world, get acquainted with the crew, and have a wonderful experience.

✇ chapter 20: the official host

"You can be whatever you want in this world if you work single-mindedly toward the goals you set for yourself."

Johnny Faevelen, Master (Captain) Norway

On a calm day, "driving a ship" and driving a car might seem an equal piece of cake. Just hit the power switch and steer. Guests know better, and they respect the fact that they entrust their safety and pleasure to professional mariners. Just how this occurs makes for interesting reading seldom considered when booking a cruise. Consider the weather, maintenance, special marine skills, and language and coordination issues with folks from many countries.

It helps to understand the cruise business, starting with the marine side, for without that, you might as well book a hotel. The captain and his sailors get you to the promised port safely and in a timely manner. They have quite the complex vehicle to get you there, too, even without considering the weather. The cruise business is like crossing the Royal Navy with a hotel, and the off-spring is a floating resort that can take you from place to place.

As with any ship, crew members have specific responsibilities. But the business of hiring, training, and coordinating the activities of those who operate such a complex vehicle requires organizational skills. Management considers its mission accomplished when guests lack awareness of the details of how this happens.

The hotel side can do its job so much better if the ship seems like a land-based hotel, steady and trustworthy, regardless of weather conditions. The master and his crew see that the hotel team can perform their mission once the sailors perform theirs.

Though the Royal Caribbean International structure has most of the elements of a private or corporate business, the operation of the ship depends on a chain of command that looks a lot like the operation of a navy ship. In emergencies, the discipline and training add to the safety and comfort of all on board. The captain must blend the requirements of the business world with the need for discipline and a command structure.

What a treat to meet Captain Johnny Faevelen, the fisherman who became captain of the largest cruise ship in the world. The vista from the bridge gives you a feeling of power and grandeur, with its closely spaced window-washing jets atop the curved glass, and the translucent shades pulled down in direct sunlight.

The ship's bridge and high-tech control room enclose a range of computers and monitors that would make NASA feel at home. The ship, so technically advanced, means a single operator waits for a computer signal from one of several thousand monitored systems alerting him to any issue that might arise. He does not have to check for "normal."

Following Dad's sea dreams

"Trust yourself," said Captain Johnny's father, Edward. "And remember," he added, "you can be whatever you want in this world if you work single-mindedly toward the goals you set for yourself."

Quoting Captain Johnny, "This was what I dreamed of as a child while standing beside my father in his small shrimp boat in the northern fjords. Young boys along the Norwegian coast have dreamed throughout all time. More than anything else, many of us wanted to go to sea. We dreamed of sailing on an open sea under a broad, broad sky, experiencing foreign ports and countries. The high point of the dream was to end up as skipper of one's own ship." The dream has come true for Captain Johnny. Those non-seamen among us think the captain's job involves driving this big vessel, but we should think again. He has people like the chief engineer, environmental officer, staff captain and many others who direct the complex operations aboard.

The captain cares deeply about his crew and guests, whether they face a calm day or a hurricane. His people, like those throughout the ship, come from everywhere, and he likes it that way, so his leadership becomes the glue that welds the human team as tight as the steel welds that keep the hull together. Speaking of the hull, consider that, during the planning stage, this miracle of man's boldness depended on input from the captain and his team to advise architects and shipyard folks, adding their experience to the design and construction of their future home. Many of the sailors aboard had navy experience somewhere along the line.

Norway: All the Alta Igloo Hotel is made of ice, except the deerskin sleeping bag.

Captain Johnny, as the visible and symbolic host for the guests, hears hundreds of compliments each week. If you asked the captain when he thought the magic of Royal Caribbean International really started, he will likely mention 1988, when the Norwegian interests passed to the current leadership of the line. Gradually, the personnel became more international, and although some very experienced Norwegians remain, the leaders welcomed the concept of cultural diversity that has become its hallmark, the envy of every great corporation.

Ironically, Norwegian tax laws and regulations led to the ownership change and new management and growth of this firm under American leadership.

He states, "For tax reasons, the Norwegians were squeezed out...We were under the Norwegian flag, and very proud of it, but the Norwegian Maritime Law [was restrictive], and the taxation of companies in Norway was extremely high; there was no benefit for the company registering under the Norwegian flag. We could not serve beer to the crew members because in Norway when you were on board working on a ferry, or a passenger-carrying vessel, you, as an employee, couldn't serve beer or alcohol to them.

"Can you imagine a dear friend from Jamaica not being able to get a Red Stripe for eight months?"

For the most part, sailing involves calm seas. The captain steps in when weather challenges arise, and he communicates confidence to guests so the crew doesn't take the heat.

"I don't leave them out there having to deal with the problems if we have a hurricane or storm. They are not the ones that should get those questions. I should be proactive and tell the guests why we have to skip the port or change the itinerary. So, yes, that's a little bit about management style."

Top management sets the pattern, and like other key managers aboard, the captain feels he has the confidence and support of headquarters management, and they let him build and encourage his team with freedom to act, grow, and innovate. The reader who has sailed with a Royal Caribbean International captain knows from experience how steady and smooth the modern cruise vessel moves. The English poet, James Flecker, captured that feeling as he wrote, *"I have seen old ships sail like swans asleep."*

chapter 21: the man behind the man

"It's very important to have trust in a huge team."

Mikael Palmroos, Staff Captain, Finland

The Marine team includes a second in command, or staff captain, Mikael Palmroos, who helped in building the ship. He found it amazing to see things come together, literally, at the shipyard. At the site, the personnel included mostly Finns, with some Norwegians, but the subcontractors contributed key parts from all corners of the world. Friction among cultures has no place in shipbuilding, since the contractor receives payment only if the product delivers on time, operates true to the drawing, and works as expected.

"I went to Finland early with the new build team. Since I have the experience from being in operation with the ship, when you put those two things together, you have a new ship. You also have to have new operational procedures for this type of ship. You try to have somebody that is actually building a ship to try to get them to understand what we need as mariners out here, and why we need it. They use hundreds of subcontractors from different parts of the world to get the thing together. So, you work again with a lot of different nationalities at the yard itself," says Mikael.

"Set your course by the stars, not by the lights of every passing ship." **Omar Bradley**

He loves to sail the ship and spent a compulsory year in the Navy of Finland before getting a degree in Sweden. Mikael worked the ferries in Scandinavia and worked as an able seaman on cargo ships. He loves interacting with guests while he walks about the ship. He likes to talk about the ship's loyalty ambassador, a former rodeo barrel racer, because she has so many fans who love to see her on repeat cruises. The marine officers get ten weeks on and ten off, so he has the chance to build crew relationships with people of many countries and can visit them in interesting places, mentioning the Maldives as a recent trip. This sailor can operate smaller boats as well. He participated on the Finnish team at the European championships in kayaking! Crews of various ships compete at ports of call in sports like football (soccer), and he mentioned playing soccer weekly on board with crew members at the on-board basketball venue.

Crews from this and other lines compete in soccer

You might notice when he walks the ship that he has four stripes on the shoulder, and he recalls that the hotel director and chief engineer also have those, while the captain actually has a wider fourth stripe that denotes a higher rank. Other people aboard have three, two and one stripe, but you never feel the crew places importance on rank, when it comes to the satisfaction of the guest. Mikael blends the feeling about diversity with the need for safety and teamwork, saying, "I think it's very important for any type of rank, or any type of culture, to really respect and treat the others as a family. My primary function on board is, of course, to make sure we are safe and secure. So, the safety aspect for me, and the security aspect, is to develop a system for everybody to take the pride in being at the safety training. [Everyone should be] trying to understand the emergency duties, and if my neighbor is not a hundred per cent sure, [I want to] be able to support that team member or bring up the concern. It's very important to have trust in a huge team."

Mikael also talks about the bubble. People inside any "in group," like an ethnic or other group with similar kinds of people, feel like a bubble encloses them, and they may or may not look outside. Those who feel open to other cultures get outside that bubble, learn, and expand their knowledge. With respect to leadership training and styles, Mikael likes the "Building on Talent" program, which, for a week, by invitation, includes ways for managers to share information about their specialty with different people. He described the four pillars of financials, crew satisfaction, safety, and guest relations, and believes those who see the big picture will become more understanding of the various cultures and the way people develop in different ways.

In response to a question about hurricanes, Mikael advised that the ship either stay in port or deviate around them.

The marine team knows about shows outside in the Aqua-theatre, and they adjust course to accommodate activities on board, working closely with all the crew members on the hotel side.

chapter 22: keep the resort humming

"We make sure we respect each other."

Stig Eriksen, Chief Engineer, Norway.

If you ever get the chance to talk to a chief engineer, take it! Near Stig Eriksen's office, you see signs for a chief refrigeration engineer, and an electrical engineer, etc.

Modern technology at work

You could count nearly a hundred crew members, just in the engine department. Stig grew up in a coastal town of about 8,000 people, got a maritime education, and joined the Royal Navy, signing with Royal Caribbean International about fifteen years ago.

He believes the people you meet on board become your friends, and you learn to work with all nationalities. "You know a chief engineer on board any ship really in the modern world is basically a right-hand captain on the technical side. We are more or less very similar in education and such. You know, the start of it is very similar: the nautical side goes this direction. He becomes the captain. I go the technical way, and I become the chief engineer."

Monitors everywhere

Stig gets involved with the hotel side as well. "There is an enormous world out there just to support the electrical side of it. Just to make sure that all the lights are on all the venues. Like when you go to the theatre today; it's more than just an on and off switch. The systems are getting so complicated these days. Same thing with the engine room today."

Behind the scenes, Stig insists that his people respect and understand each person, regardless of their culture. The ship has its own culture, helping overcome the challenge of ethnic diversity. He took new crew on a tour.

"I had some discussion when I went to a dining room a couple of days ago, and they were fascinated that one they meet is from Indonesia, the next guy they talk to is from Trinidad and Tobago. They [the experienced staff] still provide the exact same service but they know that, the cultures are totally different. I'm not saying it's the biggest challenge, but it's definitely something that has a very high focus, making sure that the crew that joins the ship, especially new joiners, understand how we operate, and adapt to the culture with how we support them. They need to understand that this is the product we want to provide. That goes not only for the hotel staff that is in front of the line. It's just as important behind the scenes, where we have cooks. Just in the engine room, we are probably about seven, eight different nationalities. So it goes, everywhere you walk on the ship; I would say you almost never meet two from the same country. With seventy-nine cultures represented, chances are slim."

Table with detailed deck schematics

He knows that some cultures revere the elderly. Stig's age could work against him elsewhere, but at Royal Caribbean International, he earns respect on merit, though younger than most Chief Engineers.

He took over at age twenty-eight and supervised a mixture of crew ages.

"When I was first promoted I was probably the youngest chief leader at the time. Ten years ago, when I took over as chief engineer and, you know, with my age then and the diversity of the crew on board, it could've been a challenge, but with the mix of crew that we had, it worked extremely well. It also comes down to who you are as a person."

He said, "Obviously, it comes through the way we put together training programs. It comes in the way we put activities on board, behind the scenes activities, crew activities, and the way we all respect each other. I think that's the key to the success. We make sure we respect each other."

Stig's concern with possible age discrimination ties back perfectly to this book's reporting about cultural discrimination. The problems in areas involving age and gender are treated differently in many parts of the world. The solution he notes is the same as the ones the crew reports for language, cultural diversity, and ethnic discrimination: respect, lubricated by smiles and greetings.

Monitors alert exceptions to normal

Each new crew member takes a two-week training course for "familiarization", but they supplement that formal training with supervisor counseling about life aboard ship, leading to a maturing experience. Mikael believes your responsibility extends to your own activities, on or off the ship at ports of call.

The current fully trained crew might appear strong and self-confident but intimidating to a new person.

He believes communication goes both ways, openly. If part of the crew looks overworked, others pitch in to help.

He also gave the example of the third engineer, whose mom got sick, and the ship arranged for him to get home the next day.

1,800,000 saunas in Finland: population is 5,000,000.

He and the crew will put all their strength into helping out.

Management arranged all flight connections, and no one said that they would finish lunch first before making the arrangements.

A trust exists that each team member will find help in time of need.

Today, on this big ship, there exists a trained care team, whereas on smaller ships you would expect volunteers to help.

Stig's message to guests concerns acceptance of an amazing life experience that permits them to meet many people in a fine environment.

Speaking of trust, he says, with respect to the Miami headquarters, "They always have time to listen to you.

There's always room for improvement and discussions. The information goes both ways. I think that's probably one of the keys to success within the marine operation, that there's research and the open communication between the office and the ships."

Stig does not sit still.

"I think if you walk through a day, and you probably meet a hundred people on the way, you will find that over ninety of them have smiles on their faces and that's fascinating."

When you take your next cruise, think about the folks that take you safely from place to place.

They each have their families and interests, (Stig's include daughters, four and eight) and they might share a few additional stories with you if you stopped to talk.

You just might get an invitation to their hometown to see through their eyes what tourists don't see.

"On one ship, a guy worked in the incinerator room, and he was a podiatrist."

Tyler Ince, Marketing and Revenue Manager, USA

With respect to the hotel side, suppose someone asked you to operate, profitably, a floating hotel with 8,000 guests aboard. Perhaps the first task involves organizing hundreds of people into a skilled team. But a hotel, in this case, can't look like a static enclosure containing beds and bathrooms. It should please the guests and entice them to come back again soon. It should plan for different ages, genders, languages, and cultural tastes in food and entertainment. That plan needs to serve the basic creature comforts and needs for everything from health to clean clothes and linens. The plan needs sizzle. It needs to make the experience fun, educational, entertaining, and rewarding.

Spreadsheet guru

The word "hotel" limits the imagination.

When you look at the seven neighborhoods featured on *Allure of the Seas* or *Oasis of the Seas*, or the amenities on other modern cruise ships, you must describe a rather complete resort and entertainment venue.

Tyler Ince, the Marketing and Revenue manager, has a computer screen as big as your living room TV on which marches every piece of data you could imagine.

Want to know how many Corona Cigars they sold in the bar on deck five between 4:00 p.m. and 5:00 p.m.? You will know the answer in ten seconds.

Ride operator: It's the "big kids" you must look out for

Interesting guy. Tyler explains that cruise fares have changed little in the past few years, even dropping, while costs of living rise every year.

So how does a cruise line survive? The secret may lie in his carefully managed spreadsheets which chronicle the discretionary "extras" that the weekly captive audience chooses to enjoy, whether they involve food, communication, gambling, or recreation.

Tyler received his business degree at Texas Tech and MBA at University of South Carolina, a school that has 100 of 150 people from other countries. He began his career in New York and, somehow, along the way, managed to give a speech on diversity at Beirut University. Tyler grew up in Dallas, learned Spanish, and spent time in Croatia at fifteen.

The marketing and revenue manager gets deeply involved in guest satisfaction (the activities provided to guests) and business (the income streams that allow the cruise line to pay its people, build new ships, and offer desired services.)

140 US towns have "Christmas" in their names.

As guests, you take for granted that photos show up in a picture wall or your personal folder shelved on a tall numbered carousel or in a computer screen for you to place an order.

Photographers appear at every ship activity. You see them in restaurants and at events in the evenings with special backdrops for picturing taking. Within hours, those pictures are processed for viewing in those personal folders as well as in a whole room set aside with walls of photographs divided by activity.

Before entering the ship on the first day your photograph is taken and used for computerized facial recognition to distinguish who you are.

You assume the spa, casino, and recreation areas will have answers for your needs. You expect exercise and entertainment opportunities.

Tyler knows the exact number of crew members from Kenya (1) or Trinidad and Tobago (54) during this week's cruise.

The printout shows seventy-nine nationalities, with the top three as Filipino, Indian, and Jamaican, followed by 138 persons from Indonesia and 120 from St. Vincent and the Grenadines.

What does Tyler do between contracts? Guests wonder about such things. Crewmates know much about their homelands and proudly share their knowledge while encouraging Tyler to visit on his time away from the ship.

"I went to ten countries in ten weeks and I never spent a day alone. I pulled into Romania and Bucharest. I've got my friend who's the restaurant manager picking me up from the airport. Another friend tells me, 'If you are in Romania, you call me. Within five minutes, I'll have an assistant waiter there to make sure you're okay,' because he knows somebody in every city in Romania. So, anywhere I went in Romania, I knew I was okay, and then I cross the border and

I make it to Bulgaria. I've got another friend, he picks me up puts me on a bus, sends me to meet up with another guy, the facilities manager on *Oasis*. I meet him. He drives me back with his wife and his kid," Tyler explains.

Stories like this imply a certain atmosphere and a team spirit on a ship that finds a management specialist hosted in these countries by friends on board. These friends care enough to show off their city and country to him.

In this context, it seems unimportant that a person has a different religion from yours. The world's leaders might consider counting to ten, or even higher, before starting a war over religion or politics if their citizens could see and better understand the world by befriending someone from a different culture.

Tyler says, "I was in Lebanon with people from ships, so I actually ended up speaking on cultural diversity and international [relations] to the American University in Beirut."

As a traveler, of course, you can take tours. You will sleep where the guides designate and see the standard sights. However, suppose you took a bit of time with the waiter to ask about the country on his badge, and you learned enough to get interested. He or she might tell you about some fascinating places in their hometowns that the tourist doesn't normally see on the "one country each day" bus.

Tyler saw Turkey with the help of the chef from an *Allure* specialty restaurant: Chops. He's planning a visit to Munich for Oktoberfest with the head chef from Germany.

Tyler manages about 200 people. The revenue from the cruise ticket, which used to account for eighty percent of the guest's outlays, now accounts for a lower percent, in part because the ticket prices have remained low while costs have increased. A cruise week, with food and entertainment, costs about the same as a NY hotel room for a weekend.

Tyler dated a shipmate from Gozo, Malta. Most of us couldn't find some of the crew members' countries on a map! This ship's crew might have less diversification (speaking only English and their home country's language) than the ships in Europe where they need more language skills.

Tyler says, "I got my casino manager who is British military. He was stationed at Checkpoint Charlie when that wall came down, and he's got a great story. He lives in South Africa because he met a girl on a ship from South Africa."

Talk to the crew and get a world tour.

Tyler saw new guests asking directions to their seating assignment and stopped to assist. They mentioned a certain server they liked on another ship, the *Oasis* last year. Tyler phoned the headwaiter, asked about Tatyana, and arranged for seating at her table! It's quite often the *people* that distinguish a cruise line.

The diversity thing doesn't stop at ethnicity. Cruise employees started their careers with occupations dramatically different from their current choice on the ship.

"On one ship, a guy worked in the incinerator room, and he was a podiatrist back in Central America. He made more money working on the ship than being a doctor back home. There was a Somalian who had a PhD in Physics on ships in India. The guy was brilliant, and he's selling wine on the cruise ships in the dining room because it was a better opportunity for him."

Royal Caribbean International has assembled a fascinating array of folks you pass by daily. You have the chance to learn about their homes and cultures in Europe, Asia, South America, Africa, and the South Seas. They come to you, at your table and stateroom, and they will delight you if you take an interest in their lives and learn about the world, person by person.

The crew itself may come from Croatia or Serbia, and work together on a common task of pleasing the guest, while their relatives at home remain somewhat uncooperative with people from other countries.

Tyler talked about a new plan to offer more on-board excursions. "Guests want to see the laundry. They're fascinated by how we do laundry for 8,000 people.

They want to see the galley. How do we make all this food for 8,000 people? You're talking about 30,000 meals a day.

They want to see the engine room and the bridge. They want to see the crew bar. All of these places, the crew gym. People are saying that those are the best tours they've taken."

Royal Caribbean International thinks of those less fortunate. The British press may have had a field day taunting Royal Caribbean International about docking at a Haitian port with its wealthy passengers a day after the earthquake. Better journalism might have brought out the fact that many pallets of food, and supplies came immediately, thanks to Royal Caribbean International, the first boat to dock after the tragedy. They should have mentioned this line "adopted" Haiti for help by crew and corporation.

Charities like Make-a-Wish Foundation benefit continuously with raffles (over $16,000 raised in June on one ship) and donation cards for guests and crew on all ships one month each year. This speaks volumes for their good citizenship from top to bottom. The crew alone contributed to "Make-a-Wish" the tidy sum of $3,652 in one week.

"Crew helping crew" stories keep coming. Spontaneous collections to get a member home to deal with a tragedy regularly raise $500 to $1,000 for that needed plane ticket, given with care for the need without hesitation. The Casino crew gave $100 each when one of their own had a severe need. The world offers us constant challenges, and a cruise ship represents the world. **The guests and the crew have diverse backgrounds, and Tyler takes advantage of the fact that these many citizens of many nations have come together in a spirit of curiosity and cooperation to work, learn, and make new friends.**

🦅 chapter 24: so they can eat and drink

"We're constantly upgrading and evolving our offerings."

Marcus Juen, Food & Beverage Manager, Austria

Marcus came from Austria, but now lives in England. His career with Royal Caribbean International spans almost twenty years now, and he enjoys it, especially on this ship. He describes it as the biggest and the best, and his group represents the biggest division on board. His 1,073 people, working within food & beverage, contribute to the biggest percentage of the various nationalities. He remarked that some of the countries represented are at war with each other.

Crew mess has ethnic food diversity

The different religions, beliefs, and traditions, according to Marcus, "just mold together."

Lettuce taking a bath

"I think there's a mutual understanding to respect each other and to work together. It's also amazing for me to talk to my staff as well to find out about their backgrounds.

We might have waiters on board who used to be lawyers or doctors and everything else. Since we have so many ships, it's great to see people you haven't seen in years and all of a sudden, you work here in the same ship and you meet up again."

Chopped to bite size and dried

Starting in Austria, he apprenticed at a hotel school. Marcus observes, "If anybody needs financial assistance, our guys are probably the first ones to pitch in and collect some money for those people, regardless of nationality or anything like this.

Ready for the salad bowl assembly

We're like a family around here, and I don't mean in a cordial cheesy way. You know it's really true. Everybody understands what might be acceptable, what is common in one place, and what might be offensive to another nationality. You have crew members from completely different corners of the world who literally become best friends, develop a romantic relationship, and get married.

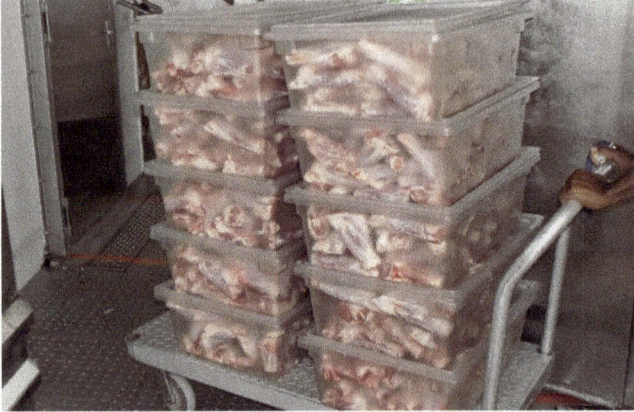

Meat ready for the Chef's magic

We have our standard recipes for our operation. Of course, we also have our crew mess where all the crew and staff officers have their meals.

We probably have a little more food diversity over there even than what we put out to our guests because of the various nationalities. We try to cater to all of them obviously.

We have somebody who has his or her favorites and likes and dislikes. It doesn't mean that an Indian person only cooks Indian food."

Sliced to perfection

Marcus feels very fortunate being with the company for so long and seeing some of the most beautiful places. "It's been quite a good ride."

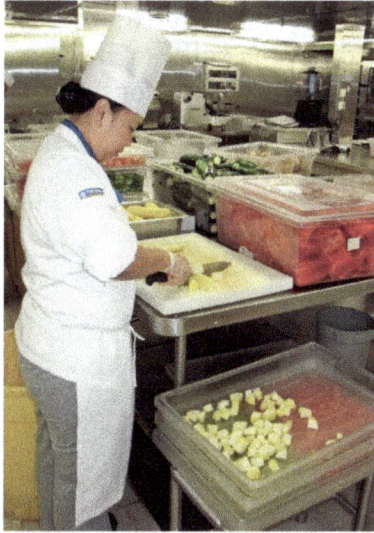

Cutting squash for stir-fry dish

"Do you get homesick for some of the things from Austria?" I ask.

"You always look forward to your mom's cooking; it's always going to be special, but I am quite international when it comes to my own cooking. We are constantly upgrading and evolving our offerings and see which dishes are more popular than others. And we do reviews and change a lot of our items, probably twice a year as a fleet. It's also done by our corporate chef, and, of course, every so often, we change our menu.

"What I like to accomplish at least twice a day is to be in every single one of my areas of responsibility to see how it's going, to touch base with some of the crew members working over there, seeing what's going on, what's happening. Then of course, I'm happy if I can keep up with my emails. There is a lot of office work, but I would much rather just go out there and say hello to people.

Austria: only continental EU country not a NATO member.

"We have great crew facilities here. We have different bars and recreational rooms where we can go after work. The mess is open to everyone. There's no segregation or different areas for different ranks or anything, so it's great. We do all kinds of celebrations because our people are proud of the places where they're from, and, of course, if it's a big national holiday, we try to celebrate with them. But all those parties are always an open invitation to any country or any nationality to attend. We also try, from a management point, to contribute to their parties by allowing them to prepare their own food like in their own traditional ways, and we allow them to do that."

You get the sense that this combination of home and work for a melting pot of cultures works out well for Marcus and for those under his supervision.

🎬 chapter 25: it's all about having fun

"When are you going to quit and get a real job?"

Ken Rush, Cruise Director, USA

Few people have the luxury of tracking down Ken Rush in his office and asking if he has a twin on board (he is seen everywhere). He works early and late. Guests think they know what he does, but after twenty-six years in the industry, and the thousands of happy people he has seen, Ken has a different perspective on his mission than anyone else. Asked about the diversified crew, he says, "Maybe what the whole world needs is to go on a cruise to see how it's done. But it is true, I mean everyone is here to have a wonderful time, and our hiring partners, who have hired these great people around the globe, have talked to them about what we're expecting in regard to the cultural diversity and about how they need to make sure that they respect each other's traditions."

Iced tea was first served at 1904 St. Louis World's Fair.

Ken told us that Jamaicans always remind him that one word sums it all up. The word: "respect." His mission? People aboard should have fun, and the only true vote for that accomplishment occurs when they return. He loves the multinational team he has working for and with him. Many of the performers have historically come from America, but he now lists many countries for his staff. He takes pride in the work Royal Caribbean International does for Haiti and several charities, and in the support given by the crew of each ship for these projects.

When asked about what he wanted to do at the beginning of his career, Ken ticked off a bunch of things: he wanted to be an actor, a TV announcer, etc. After the final night of the cruise, when he impersonated John Travolta, we concluded he had his wishes granted in all their forms!

He put a different twist on the sacred mission of pleasing guests. He said, "There is a great book out there I have never read, but the title, which I love, is, 'The Customer Comes Second,' because if your staff and crew are not happy, the customer will never be happy, so a very, very good title.

"People ask me when I do want to leave? When are you going to quit and get a real job?"

"I say, 'Are you kidding me?' I say this is a real job, and this is a dream job, because although it's hard work, everybody loves being here. You know you wake up every morning, you walk down the halls, whether it be with the guest or with the crew, and it's a good feeling. So why would I want to go anywhere else? My mom and dad said I was born for this job without a doubt. And it happened by accident when mom and dad took me and my sister and my two grandmothers on a cruise. My brother was away at school. I said, yeah, I kind of like it. I said I should talk to somebody [those in charge of hiring], and I did."

Ken may have the "real job" that makes the most money for Royal Caribbean International. For his mission involves persuading every guest to return to cruise again. And those return tickets represent the life blood of the business of cruising.

\clubsuit chapter 26: housekeeping on a large scale

"When the rating comes, we either cry or celebrate."

Lucas Chvostek, Housekeeping Manager, Czech Republic

Not one, but three, housekeeping managers care for the temporary housing needs of guests on this floating hotel. Lucas Chvostek joined Royal Caribbean International in January 2011, just after *Allure of the Seas* made its Atlantic crossing after construction. He came from the Czech Republic, where he gained experience in the hospitality industry, and then he moved to Florida in 1998 to work in hotels until his move to *Allure of the Seas*. He speaks four languages and supervises five people directly, each with twenty stateroom attendants. His team for decks ten through seventeen keeps the rooms ship-shape with a hundred persons fully trained. Though they all get some time off in the early afternoons, they work long hours, from early morning to quite late at night. In Europe, he thought a 770 room Marriott seemed like a big deal.

Crew does talent shows: jokes to ballet

When he first asked about the cycle of cleaning rooms aboard ship, imagine his amazement when he was told that the cleaning crew turns them around on Sunday a.m. in four or five hours. For the typical hotel with a number of persons checking out and in, cleaning only a few rooms seems feasible. Lucas tells about his initial expectations, coming aboard to manage a huge staff.

40% of Czech land is farmland.

On his first turnaround day on ship, Lucas said, "Okay we're going to reach the port in the morning. We'll probably stay in the port for two or three days for the ship to be cleaned and stocked. Then they told me, 'No, we're reaching the port at six o'clock and around one o'clock, 6,000 people are coming back on the ship.' I was, like, how can that be possible? That's just impossible. Each week, crew members leave, and others come aboard. From ten to twenty leave each week on the housekeeping team of 300, so training continues weekly. When crew members come on board, they are required to undergo three weeks of training on top of their regular jobs. They have much to learn, a challenge for Lucas as well. Sometimes he helps with counseling. When you work on a cruise ship, you have to feel the passion, and it either makes or breaks you.

"This is my second contract on this ship, but you never know, you can go on vacation, and you can return to find you've been assigned to a different ship."

When asked about crew activities, Lucas said, "We do have crew activities. There is also a calendar that comes to the crew quarters at the beginning of the month, and HR, and the training development managers are very proactive people. And they try to do a lot of crew activities, so, two weeks ago, we had people do their own thing. Some of the crew were playing music. Some of them were singing, dancing, doing ballet, or telling jokes. The management does a lot of stuff for the crew."

With respect to evaluations, Lucas commented, "Every Saturday each guest room gets a comment card. They rate stateroom cleanliness, attendants, and dining. Everything is put to the system, and then every Sunday we're just waiting for the ratings. And when the rating comes, we either cry or celebrate.

chapter 27: mind the gaps

These people only eat flowers. What am I going to serve them?"

Marina Esteves, Concierge, Brazil

In a small business, often the owner is the one who minds the gaps. He steps in when something gets overlooked, a deadline approaches, or a fix is required. In a huge operation like Royal Caribbean International, you need a "Marina." A concierge from South America, Marina Esteves, takes care of those special things for guests that come up outside the normal course of their cruise.

Multiple cultures inside one helpful gal

Three concierge crew members serve the many suites, more than the usual one or two such crew positions per smaller ship. The creativity and imagination needed as a concierge simply fits the solution to the problem, and happy guests result. Marina completed a contract at sea with guest relations, took time off to cruise as a passenger, and then realized she missed the experience on board. She applied again, then joined as a concierge, and loves it. She reports, "My family is Italian, Spanish, Danish, and Portuguese, so all my great grandfathers came from different countries in the world and met in Brazil. We always joked that they met in a carnival. I don't think so. My family is very reserved."

With respect to the interaction with crew, she observes, "Everybody needs to be sociable after working so many hours a day. Sometimes, even though you're tired, you'll still go to the crew bar and sit by a table, and someone will come and talk to you. You will meet people that work with you along the way. So being a group on board is very important, if not the most important thing for you at sea. You are far away from your family. You are far away from every-body, from your friends. Even though internet is a great thing, it still doesn't get too close, as close as you wish, to your family and friends. So, you bond with your shipmates, and this is for me one of the most wonderful things."

Sao Paulo has most Japanese people, outside Japan.

She had an experience with a group of guests with special dietary needs that tested her creativity and knowledge of where to get help on board. "When this group came on board, they already had everything prearranged. I just had to arrange for them to see a couple of shows. They had all restaurants booked and everything. They go to Rita's Cantina the first night of the cruise. Then, funny, the restaurant manager, she calls me, 'Marina, do you have any information about one of these persons in the party of sixteen being vegan? These people [vegans] only eat flowers, what am I going to serve them?"

This story has a happy conclusion and ended with grateful guests, but, in between, getting the word out to food people all over the ship was a challenge! Marina relies on her smile, and her passion for pleasing people, as well as a knack for finding solutions, to keep her guests happy, each crew member's first goal.

🦅 chapter 28 : a husband at work

"We do everything for them."

Fernando Ugalde, Concierge, Mexico

A concierge from Mexico, Fernando Ugalde had a rich history of hospitality positions and hotel education and experiences prior to his shipboard duty.

A multi-cultured marriage team

"I'm a suite concierge on board *Allure of the Seas*. I work along with another concierge. His name is Diego. We take care of the suites occupied by our Diamond Plus members and all the VIPs coming aboard. We do everything for them.

Whatever they need, that's what we do. It doesn't matter what [well obviously, except for a lot of restrictions on board]. That's the main part of the job. Obviously, we must socialize with them. They get to know us, and we get to know them also. So sometimes, we become friends. They write us from home and let us know what their needs are, and basically that's what I do."

A Mexican zacahuil (tamale) is three feet: weighs 250 pounds.

The concierges serve eighty suites and over 100 Diamond Plus members.

❦ chapter 29: a wife at work

"I will refer a Spanish-speaking guest to my husband!"

Hristina Ugalde, Guest Services Officer, Bulgaria

This guest services officer from Bulgaria polished her human relations skills in her teens as an assistant to a world-famous archeologist (her late father) while traveling the world. She also worked as a gem and jewelry sales person and as a classical music entertainer. She confessed that helping people has become her passion, and she loves her work.

Longest lasting fog (29 days), 1948, Sofia, Bulgaria

Hristina Ugalde works cooperatively with her husband, Fernando Ugalde. These two ambassadors of good will toward guests have something in common, besides their employer. They met aboard ship and became Mr. and Mrs. Ugalde! Through foresight and necessity, Royal Caribbean International takes advantage of the talents offered by couples who love the call of the sea. A hospitality business that fails to access this valuable resource misses some rare opportunities.

Hristina Uvalde commented that because of the long contracts that would keep crew members away from home, those qualified land-based spouses without children would naturally consider joining the crew to join their husbands and wives. The Ugaldes represent a microcosm of the premise of the Royal Caribbean International story. They come from two continents and cultures, and yet they work together. Though their languages differ (she speaks Bulgarian, and he speaks Spanish), they have a common language of English and a common goal through their work. They deal with persons from many nations, and often she will refer a Spanish-speaking guest to her husband, while she gets his Russian-speaking referrals, plus some of those additional folks that speak the other five languages they have between them.

They have become problem solvers: he with the suite guests, and she with both suite and stateroom guests. The roles differ slightly in that the suite guests ask about favors that will please them. The guest relations crew work behind the desk specializing in the special amenities for those in suites. Before accepting her current assignment, Hristina worked in guest relations. She described the daily challenges there of facing dozens of guests with problems and said the job calls for a "happy and a let-go person to be able to spend time there for long. You have to know how to deep breathe." Hristina knows how to smile and take a breath.

The Royal Caribbean International crew treats fellow crew, as well as guests, as individuals, without regard to rank, cultural background, or whether a guest paid a thousand dollars or several times that much to board the ship. When a guest calls at 3:00 a.m. reporting a lost wallet, the crew helps, and the search begins at once. Each guest deserves that special feeling on departure that he or she had the best possible vacation. Fernando's background in hotel work and Hristina's background in challenges while helping her father as he conducted archeology classes in Greece and the Balkans and elsewhere (where he found priceless artifacts from several centuries B.C.), give the Ugaldes a huge advantage in problem solving.

Hristina notices that Americans will share pictures of their families and other personal stories, whereas persons from some other countries may act more reserved. This gave clues as to how she and her husband, experienced guest-relations specialists, adjusted their communication to the cultures of the guests.

A nice example of the beneficial influence Royal Caribbean International offers on old prejudices includes a thought about people from Turkey or Bulgaria. In their home countries, Turks and Bulgarians might act less friendly to strangers due to historical and political factors. Because working on a cruise ship requires staff get along with people of other nationalities, those who cannot adjust to employer policies may end up looking elsewhere for employment. Therefore, crew members of all nationalities must learn to treat their fellow workers and guests as individuals, not as representatives of "governments." The politics and religion back home cease to have relevancy to the task. The absence of a lot of TV and other jarring stimulation on board also helps the atmosphere. When asked what happens to crew members when they rotate back home between contracts, Fernando and Hristina agreed that each had changed for the better in social contacts not related to work, and traditional prejudices and attitudes became a habit of the past, not useful in their current contacts back home.

A few years ago, an African had come to Hristina's home country for medical education, and locals saw the person as different, so the locals offered a cool welcome [unfriendly]. Now, she says, the colorful kids on the street seem to belong, despite the conservative nature of her people. So, it would seem that this world, with all its faults, might offer hope for tolerance and respect.

The Ugaldes expect to visit their home in Varna, Bulgaria, between contracts.

They know that as the break-time ticks by for several weeks, they will get restless, start e-mailing their friends on board, and itch to get back to the excitement of their mission

chapter 30: resort with an operatic bartender

"So just be yourself."

Perestrelo Frederico, Beverage Department, Portugal

Serves music: salsa or opera

If the goal of Royal Caribbean International depends on bringing vacationers back, remembering a guest's preferences will help make that happen. Food and beverage department personnel need to be "people people" and love their work. The beverage crew includes a mixer of drinks who sang in Europe's opera houses and who owned hotels. With the economy and stress in Portugal, Perestrelo Frederico now lives his dream aboard Royal Caribbean International ships and loves it, calling himself a "cook with drinks." Each "cook" has his tricks. Perestrelo learned discipline, like a high-performance athlete, studying opera and languages, speaking five languages well. He even takes time out to sing salsa and other music types in the bars with the bands. "I've played Rafael in Boheme.

I've played Troubadour in Trovatore. My operas won't be qualified as hard operas. I do more light operas like Boheme, La Traviata. That I can do." Perestrelo likes to converse with crew and guests from all over, and loves cultural traditions, including the Portuguese Fado houses. There, you eat good food while the crowd sits in respectful silence, despite the temptation to make noise with plate and fork. A good example of the language challenge took place when Perestrelo described the quiet reverence of audiences [speaking many languages] when they heard "Fado" music in Portugal. The nuances could not be translated. "Fado is not only a tradition, it's also a religion, because Fado means 'destiny.' Fado is very dramatic. It's telling stories and putting it into music. That's Fado. That's why there's a lot of respect, because it's just like an opera: very dramatic."

Largest human logo (34,000 people) helped win Portugal's bid to host Euro soccer games, 2004

He believes the secret for Royal Caribbean International includes a corporate expectation that new crew will come on board with respect for everyone.

"I think when you're going to work on board, you have to be very tolerant with religion, politics, personalities, and cultures otherwise it's not worth you moving from your country. It's been great for me. I have the ability of training my five languages every single day. So it's been a great experience, the way people think, the way people act, the way people eat. If you do not have the tolerance to understand there are different cultures, you might as well just go home, because you're going to spend a hard time on board."

Here's a tip for those who talk to a Jamaican. After you greet one, he will just say, "Hey!" This seems natural for them, so let the conversation develop beyond this greeting and get to know them better. When asked about some universal way to get started with another culture, Perestrelo advised, "If you have your personality, people understand your personality. If you understand other peoples' personality [accept people for who they are], it's easier for you to just connect. So just be yourself."

A smile always helps. When in the crew mess, Perestrelo sits down and starts to talk to people he hasn't met yet, not just choosing people he knows. This helps him learn more every day about other people. "We have people that have a lot of culture; they're well educated, but in their country, they cannot survive with all the qualifications they have. So, they have to come looking for a job, and they're willing to pick up the first shovel and dig the first hole." His advice proves the thesis of this book. Start a conversation. Learn something.

"Somehow, if you are black, if you are white, if I am small, or you are tall, we have come here to work and earn money, and at the end of the day, we are all winners if we work together."

Rogelio Luzadas, Facilities Manager, Philippines

Rogelio serves as both a supervisor of supervisors and a hands-on manager who can fix things himself, if needed. For Royal Caribbean International to keep things ship-shape, they need Rogelio Luzadas. Think about servicing a home or car. Each has many mechanical systems, and things go wrong. Imagine maintaining residences for about 8,000 people in the middle of the ocean, hurricanes and all. Suppose those residences had the latest in TV, phones, door entry systems, vacuum activated plumbing, and you have to maintain the kitchen, laundry, swimming pools, recreation/entertainment areas, and even the furniture for those 8,000 people. Those needs for maintenance require a capable crew to keep them humming. Seventy-plus cultures, working together, maintain these complex systems in a challenging environment, and you, as a guest, hardly notice that behind the scenes, someone looks after your comfort and safety every minute of your stay.

Mister Fix It

Rogelio's supervision involves daily, continuous training for his staff. He encourages flexibility while adhering to a single set of policies and procedures aboard ship. There are SQM, (safety quality management) rules and regulations, and all staff have to adapt to them. When it comes to the cultures and diversities found onboard, of course, the challenges test an individual's flexibility with people of many nationalities. "Somehow, if you are black, if you are white, if I am small, if you are tall, we have come here to work and earn money, and at the end of the day, we are all winners if we work together."

When crew members complete a contract, and they go home, managers may try to get them back to the same ship. Rogelio likes to see the return of experienced workers but sometimes he gets others. "If they are not a problem in my division, then, why not? I like to take the opportunity as long as I have it, but sometimes I cannot win all things. Sometimes, whether I like it or not, I have to take them, [rehires]. So, I teach them all the tools that they need. As a manager, also, it's important not only that you're doing your job, but that you motivate your people. It's part of my job, and it's good to see people growing up and maturing in their work."

At two, Filipino writer Jose Rizal could read and write; later spoke 20 languages.

Rogelio, like many aboard, speaks English as a second language. Guests might try to imagine reversing roles, trying to speak any language used by the cultures aboard ship. This could help them in cutting a bit of slack if the wait staff or stateroom attendant stumbles over a word.

Rogelio supervises maintenance in the hotel when it comes to carpentry, upholstery, plumbing, swimming pools, and Jacuzzis. If the stateroom or deck furniture breaks, he jumps on the case. Keeping the plumbing going would challenge anyone.

"I started as an engine trainee in 1996, the lowest position in the marine department. I learned all of this from my school. I was a mechanical engineer back home, north of Manila. After my college, and after I applied to the Royal Caribbean International hiring partner in Manila, I felt very lucky to be in the company, so I'm still here. I was a repairman, repairing laundries or swimming pools, and then there was a new position in the facilities, facilities repair supervisor, in Germany. So, they put me there." He not only supervises, but can do the work with the Jacuzzis and other things, saying, "Yes. I'll tell them [I can do any job] even if I close my eyes." A delightful way of expressing confidence in experience.

Rogelio shared his secret for motivating his team. "First thing is, if fun is there, it's always there, you have to work with them with fun, right? You have to acknowledge them, to acknowledge their good work. They make mistakes.

Mistakes are always there. Nobody is perfect, so you have to teach them, and you have to give them the tools, not only the teaching. You teach and teach, but if one guy is hard headed, is not willing to learn, of course we have these opportunity labs, procedures that we have in the SQM. SQM is like a bible of the company."

When asked about the support provided by top management, Rogelio responded by giving examples of the latest tools for communication, procedures, and technology. These tools ensure prompt and efficient repairs and very little down time. The foregoing represents a textbook case of leadership, carrot-and-stick supervision, training, and attitude adjustment, delivered with humor and patience. Many guests wonder about the unique toilet design, and Rogelio explains about the vacuum system that uses less water, does the job, saves fuel and money, and repairs quickly. Sometimes during a week, the Facilities Management department has 200 issues with toilets, whether it involves guests throwing stuff in them, or failing to push the flush buttons hard enough. Repair procedures from the electronic manuals are always up to date for each ship.

Compared to other managers, Rogelio has a slightly different situation with language issues. "In my position now, all the people working with me, we come from the same country. We are all Filipinos.

So, this time, I don't have any challenges when it comes to communication, or when it comes to cultures, but in my previous contracts, I worked with different nationalities where we had challenges when it came to their English speaking. So, what do we do with them? We put them in two-berth cabins with the good English speaking crew." He is also fortunate in another respect. "My wife is on board. I would say maybe ten percent of the crew are couples." Rogelio met his wife, a nurse, on board, about five years ago.

His favorite food is chicken adobo. After fifteen years with Royal Caribbean International, he says, "Every day is Monday," meaning that with a seven-day schedule, all days seem the same without a weekly rhythm. He explains to his wife why he does not often go on shore. He might miss a crisis on board and would be unavailable to help. Rogelio has taken out new ships on their maiden voyages eight times, saying, "We are the representatives of the company for a certain job." He inspects ships before the line accepts delivery. This seems a bit more time consuming than kicking the tires on a new car in the showroom before driving off! He states, "Yes, I'm on duty twenty-four hours. Regularly, I work ten to eleven hours a day, but my phone is always on. We have people who are twenty-four hours on duty on a shift and they know what to do. If they don't know, and it's a big problem, that's the time they have to wake me up."

Rogelio says, in effect, that the country of origin for each worker fades into the background when addressing tasks. Two workers from politically unfriendly countries find it possible to cooperate in their job mission and leave the religious and political issues at home. Their home countries have no importance on board, a critical secret to success of the mission. Many readers will discover insights from this multi-cultural miracle of cooperation and respect, and they will observe and question situations in their daily life where they see a shortage of teamwork and friendliness.

Often such insights will lead to changes in approach, like the crew member who shared the story about the ten-foot rule of friendliness with a mother who owned a beauty parlor. She tried the rule as an experiment and greatly increased her business. The ten-foot rule simply says one should smile at anyone coming within ten feet. **Rogelio exaggerates this theory as a courteous and respectful manager. Afraid of not being around in case of an emergency, he rarely leaves the ship on a day off proving his dedication to his job.**

chapter 32: keeping fit and happy

"We just have to figure out how to turn on the magic, and sprinkle it, and bring it to life."

Mitchell Merucci, Activities Manager, USA

The Activities Manager, Mitchell Merucci, described a new Activities 360 program, which just rolled out twenty new activities after much research. They plan events for all ages and many nationalities and interests. The goal remains the same. The guest will have the best vacation ever. He commented that an empty ship, or one with a crew that does not smile, would not work, for the happy crew opens the door to happy guests.

Crew lounge: they must all be at work

It would seem hard to beat the program he already supervises.

He says, "A lot of my activities are for families specifically...we have our karaoke bar, which might not attract all cultures, but it attracts a certain type. We have Boleros, which is our Latin-inspired bar. Then there's the pub, and also there's the Schooner bar (piano bar). The show-band bar and the big dance floor for the ballroom style music attract those who like to dance. There's something for everybody. The sports deck offers a running deck, basketball court, mini golf course and a surfboard area for the active, outgoing people. The spa caters to those who want to relax. Central Park is for those who just want to take a walk or listen to the birds, and the Boardwalk is for kids and families that are young at heart. All the entertainment venues: the ice rink, the theater for our Broadway performances, the casino, etc. all afford different types of fun. We just have to figure out how to turn on the magic, sprinkle it, and bring it to life.

Crew recreation area

"On these ships alone, it's a little bit different, but these ships can get up towards 50% international guests. Most guests come from the US, but we have people every week from Israel to South America, from Egypt to Iran to Russia, from China to Germany, like sixty to seventy different nationalities every week. So, we have to try and find a mix for that."

Crew dining area

Mitch gets involved with the dance and karaoke area. Just listen to the variety he offers. "I like to try and offer as much as I can to all different kinds of people. I will offer a line dance class, which is for people who might not know how to really dance, but need a little bit of basic, just for fun. They just want to try it. That's one of the old cruise ship activities. We offer shuffleboard here, of course. You have probably seen online what they call the flash mob, where all of a sudden, people just break out in a dance. We actually teach this to the guests. You'll see all the guests come, and then we teach them throughout the week. On the last day of the cruise, we do a surprise performance on the promenade, and all the guests stop and see it. That's for younger people.

Crew stays in touch with home

"We'll do Latin dance classes for those guests [interested in that venue]. In the Latin bar, we will do meringue and salsa competitions. But we're trying to cater to every kind of demographic and nationality in its own little way. We're going to teach a Lady Gaga and Michael Jackson dance class."

"We try to get all different ages taking part in the activities because, at the end of the day, when the guests leave, we want to know that they've enjoyed it. We want to try to offer all styles of dancing for all ages whether it is a family, a younger person, an older person; there is something for everybody. That is the trick because this is not just an adult resort. It is everybody from zero to ninety-five years old from all over the world.

"At our karaoke bar, we have uploads of 8,000 to 10,000 songs, in English, USA, (big artists there), plus Portuguese, Spanish, Brazilian, Italian, French, and all different styles of music."

Asked about guests from India, he responded, "I wish you would have been there yesterday. There was the World's Sexiest Man Competition. We bring the guys in one at a time, and they do a little dance to try and look sexy for those judges. It's a lot of fun. One of the guys was from India, and he was the best one by far. The crowd went insane for him—he took off his shirt, he did not care, big hairy chest and he is dancing and the crowd just went crazy, crazy for him. And it's so funny because when you say, 'coming up next', and you announce Seneo, from India, he comes out, and he's like dancing Bolliwood. He takes off his shorts. He's got like Speedo underwear on, and the crowd goes wild. You do not expect it. Most people do not know that many people from India. When you are on a cruise, part of the fun is meeting everybody from all over the world. It used to be just the crew, but now, on these ships, it is the guests as well. This ship is being advertised around the entire world.

Anyone for Bingo?

"On board, there is a TV channel for crew, special activities people to plan events for crew, a crew welfare team, and a whole set of events using the rock climbing wall and the flow rider (surf simulator), and other guest facilities at suitable times that don't conflict with guest activities.

"You'll see the crew play soccer. Some of the time, we'll play against other ships. We have big rivalries. We'll go against the Carnival ship, or whatever ship, and they'll go so far as to have jerseys made for their actual team. We have matches and bragging rights."

Mitch quoted a corporate officer as saying, "The ship is the ship, and it's beautiful, but without the crew, without you here, it's really nothing."

He talked about fitness and the advent of a "biggest loser" TV show for the crew to compete to lose weight with yoga, running, biking, and extra classes. With a huge crew of over 2,200 on board, that audience equals the guest list on most ships, and a lot of attention goes into keeping the crew happy. The Captain plays a mean game of soccer with the crew team, too.

Mitch described the training for the "ten-foot rule." If anyone, guest or crew, comes within ten feet, you are expected to greet them with "Hi," and a smile, and this seems to make all the difference in the climate aboard the ship.

Mitch described it this way, "I don't even know this guy, but I say hi to him. He is from China or Russia, but it does not matter. We still say hi. And it just creates a bond that isn't really spoken of, but you're part of a team." This formula works!

Mitch said, "I would love to know the inside framework of how they hire. I think it's a very selective process. There are hundreds of applicants every day that come through. Back in the day when I got my job, they used to conference...they would fly to India, they would fly to Toronto. When I got selected, I had to do an in-person interview panel and then one-on-one. They do not do that as much anymore because, now, there are just so many ships and so many people to hire that most interviews they can do over Skype. But whatever they do, they know what they're looking for."

Mitch has become a changed person. He says, "For us to be living this experience working together, I would say I would never take this back or would never trade off anything with this experience, because I feel so cultured now with an understanding of all the different cultures in the world. And you can see where there's a difference in each culture. And you can see how people are brought up in different parts of the world just by working with them and knowing who they are."

Juneau, Alaska: Largest US city at 3000 square miles.

Each weekend, Royal Caribbean International trades about 26,000 people from ship to shore and back again from a fleet of ships at Ft. Lauderdale. Every one of those people will have a life-changing experience with people from every part of the world, as they pass by or talk and share things about their culture and traditions."

🦅 chapter 33: no resort without music

"I now have friends all over the world when I go to visit, not just musicians."

Josh Scalf, Musical Director, USA

The Musical Director, Josh Scalf, began his career when the 6th grade teacher needed a tuba player, showed him a tuba picture, and he decided to try out. After a fine music education in Alabama, he got some scholarships, put together bands, and talked to some Glen Miller band players visiting town and hit on the subject of bands looking into playing in a band on cruise ships. He did auditions and joined the Royal Caribbean International team.

Finding the right costume backstage

He thinks he may be the only full-time tuba player on cruise ships, but he doubles on trombone and directs the shows as well.

He started dramatically, in that he had never cruised before and flew to Rome to start work the next day on a cruise ship. On arrival, he discovered his luggage had been routed elsewhere, so he put on walking shoes and visited the Coliseum and tourist sights before joining the ship and its band. The number of countries he has traveled to from cruising along with the number of instruments he plays has helped him grow as a person and musician. Josh talked about the clarinet player who, just before the curtain, had trouble with the keys dropping from his instrument, so creative players bent them back in shape and the show went on. The show even continued when a poorly taped-down audio cord that impacted every speaker got loose during a pit rise as the overture started. After an electronic screech, the audio guy became a hero, dropping the pit players' volume and bumping up the taped track instruments so the audience never knew the performers avoided a disaster. His advice, perfect for everyday life, "There is never a 'musical emergency.'" Josh meant that no one drowned or died, and life goes on, even though the crisis may have seemed bad at the time.

One of many bands

"We have a bond as musicians, obviously, when we can interact musically on the stand, and that just helps really grow the friendships at an exponential rate. I've known these guys for maybe two and a half or three years, but I feel like I've known them half my life already."

He admired the talent of the sax player, Juan, from Buenos Aires, Argentina and said, "Our drummer was from Canada. The piano player, George, was from Bulgaria. It was the most diverse a group he had worked with.

"Throughout the rest of the musical division, we have some of the island guys doing the Calypso music stuff, the Latin band guys, I think they were from Peru when I first got on board, the strings are from Ukraine. I worked with guys from Australia who had a really, really good grasp on the fundamentals of American jazz and did a lot of the big band."

Wardrobe for on-stage characters

Josh has the attitude that the native country of a musician plays no role if they have the skill. "It's more the individual, their work ethic on their instrument, and their ability when they perform."

The theaters have lighting and "flying" apparatus opportunities and some have full stage-width, back-projection images that permit unheard of effects, as for example on *Oasis*. The shows rival those of any theater on land.

Jimmy Carter was the first president born in a hospital.

In nearly three years with Royal Caribbean International, Josh adjusts easily to the fact that some unknown person may come aboard as the new player of some instrument, but the new musician gets a half hour or more to rehearse and picks up the beat and the show begins.

Clothes fit for a king

The Royal Caribbean International "headliner performers" differ every week and come aboard for a few days to thrill the guests. The big Broadway shows, the ice, water, gymnastic and dive events, stay on board much longer.

chapter 34: what's your lucky number?

"This is the largest floating casino in the world"

Christian Able, Casino Dealer, UK

Casino expert

People who don't think the casino is important to Royal Caribbean International's business plan should ask a stock analyst to calculate the profits of the firm without it. Christian has all the expected skills, and then some. From Manchester UK to the Bahamas, and then to Royal Caribbean International, this talented guy knows the business, beginning in 1982. Part of a team of sixty-four casino workers from twenty-two nationalities, guests can call them "close," and no one will mind.

There aren't a lot of crew members to go to dinner with you when you get off work at 3:00 a.m. Turns out, their "upside down" shifts force them to get to know each other.

"This is just a job, so we're comforting each other while we're away [at sea].

There is no nastiness or arguments. We just get along, and the management is fantastic as well. They cater to parties at night," Christian says.

Christian got started on sea rather than land in 2003. He saw other lines, but has the strong belief that Royal Caribbean International ranks first, and told stories to back this up. The ship has a welfare committee for people who need help with health issues or getting home for an emergency, and when someone presents reasonable wishes, management usually grants them.

His specialty is the craps table. "I've been dealing that off and on for the last fifteen years so I know the game inside out. It is a very difficult game to learn. We have people we train. We make sure that they know the game well," he says.

Windsor Castle: oldest royal residence still used by family.

This is the largest floating casino in the world, he thinks. He has worked on nine ships, and his manager trusts the team.

Christian explains his work with craps this way, "Because it's such a difficult game to learn, once you learn it, it's very, very addictive. It is fast paced on two bases, thirty-six combinations, so you have thirty-six ways of winning at one throw. You can imagine you have ten people on either side; there's just so much going on. On Thursday, we usually have lessons from 5:30 p.m. until 6:00 p.m. You are the one who has helped them from the start, and the next thing you know, they will ask for you. They want to play at your table because they do not want to go through learning how to play again."

When asked about silly questions by guests, Christian said, "Well, the most frequent question is they think that once the casino closes, we go off boat. We're on board the ship and it's frightening sometimes because if there's a sea [bad storm], then where are we going to go? The helicopters on shore so a lot of them don't think that we're really on board. We just work for the casino and when it closes, we go." Some of the guests ask questions. Like, "I am married. May I go to the singles bar?"

Communication is constant between him and his ten and thirteen-year-old daughters back in the UK. He has great quality time with his family between contracts.

Of course, when guests lose money, it's a stressful situation. Christian thinks someone once lost about $3,000 in craps. One man lost $22,000 in a week, and Christian has heard of higher losses, but notes that those who win on Monday don't always have the same results at week's end! Odds catch up. Best advice: Be lucky!"

chapter 35: delightful cuisine

"Our motto is, out of many, one people."

Clive Palmer, Chef, Jamaica

Loves to bake

If the casino contributes directly to profit, Clive and a couple hundred of his talented chef friends contribute to the guest retention segment of the business plan. Try staying in the cruise business with lousy food! He came from a modest background, worked hard, and achieved outstanding results. Born in the small town of Manchester, Jamaica, he grew up with grandparents, since Mom had to work after Dad died at an early age. Mom helped him learn the kitchen at age ten, though he saw her only every couple of weeks. What a wonderful example of working your way up from the bottom. He loved to bake.

"I was working with one of the teachers. After leaving school, she called me back and said, 'Okay, you are a good worker in school; therefore, I want you to work with me.' So, that's where it all began. We began to do cakes for people getting married, birthdays, and anniversaries."

His maritime career started by accident. "One Sunday, coming home from church, one of my sisters said to me, 'The newspaper said that they want a chef.' I said to her, 'In Jamaica, there's a lot of people put out stuff in the newspaper." That time, I didn't even have a passport. But I do everything in a fast process. Two weeks, I get everything. I called up the agency and they said, 'Okay, you can come for interview." The rest is history.

"They called me. Then I went down to the interview. He said there is no space yet for cooks on the ship because they are full. However, if I want to go as a utility, as a cleaner, then I can change over. I said, 'Well, no problem.' I said to myself, as long as I get to go on the ship, I can change over. It was 2004, I think, in August. I boarded the ship in Barcelona. That was the exciting part. Leaving Jamaica and going to Europe was like, where am I going?"

After the excitement of the trip and finding the ship, he stayed in the utility department for only three months.

"That was August, September, October. It was November, and the ship was very busy and there were less cooks, so Chef said there was one guy as utility and applied for a cook. Then I said, 'Okay, that's me.' He said, okay."

Only world flags without red, white, or blue: Jamaica and Libya.

We point out the humble beginnings, because this chef reported in modest fashion how he concentrated on becoming a high-quality crew member, learning everything well, learning many new skills, passing numerous written tests, and rising to CDP1, [chef with higher responsibility than CDP2 or 3]. He hopes to go even a step higher on the world's largest cruise ship: a sous chef. Clive has sailed in Dubai and has seen sights his family back home could scarcely imagine.

With respect to the diverse crew, he says, "Well, you get to know a little about their culture. It's really good, because it shows you that no matter where you go, you have something alike or in common in different areas. So, most of the time you are learning what they really eat or what is their national dish. So, then, you're surprised to know that what you have in your country, they have, because they ask you about your independence or what you guys do during the Christmas. So, eventually, it's almost the same thing most people do, the same thing. They get together, their family, they eat and they celebrate." Clive's team has folks from Indonesia, China, Africa, India, Jamaica, Philippines, and Ukraine.

Clive used to seek out Jamaicans, but he now likes to mix with others. He referred to the training videos about China and South America, and the way they help crew members to avoid offending another culture. "Whenever I joke, I always say certain things, and for them [foreigners other than Jamaicans] it is no problem. When they [people other than Jamaicans] show you, you have to say, okay, you cannot say that because they take it serious. So, it's really helpful. As time goes by, then once you start to rap with different nationalities, then you know exactly what they're all about, what they're like, and what they don't like."

Asked about what he likes to cook, he responded, "I love my fruitcake. What we make in Jamaica is very strong, plenty of rum." Clive considered his career choice as a good one. "Yes, it more than meets my expectation of travel around the world free of cost. That's the advantage because number one, if I was in Jamaica, I wouldn't even think about looking on that side of the world, and I'd be in there, working with my mother in Jamaica. I always try to go in as many tours as possible just to see and take pictures."

When asked if a guest wanted to talk to him about his culture and life, would he respond? Clive said, "Yes. Most of the time, working in the Windjammer, your guest, you talk to them. They ask questions, where are you from: Jamaica. What do you do? Sometimes we bring them during the tasting time [a time when guests are invited to the kitchen], to the tasting table [samples of food for guests to experience]. They come and see what we do before they eat. And they come to taste, and they ask us in the area [questions about how we make the food]. So, they're happy."

Asked about languages, he says, "Jamaica, it's mixed. Our motto is out of many, one people. You have almost everything, different nationalities that build up Jamaica. French, Indian, Filipinos, Chinese, it's all mixed. So, you come to Jamaica, you see a mixture of people."

Even if you don't take a kitchen tour, you most certainly will experience the results of all this care and training when you lift your knife and fork aboard a Royal Caribbean International cruise ship. Compare the food and service to any five-star hotel. *Bon appetit!*

Much can be learned from the inter-cultural success of Royal Caribbean International's training and encouragement of respect between people from different backgrounds. The idea "we celebrate diversity," (repeated by the crew

members in many ways), can seep into our lives, offering a ticket to new experiences with fascinating cultures around the world.

conclusion

This is an unusual "business" book. While all managers and officers of an organization will most certainly want to know how the positive attitudes of people from the top to newly hired were encouraged, this book has universal appeal to any and all employees and even guests. Unlike books with heavy texts suitable for an MBA student, this group of stories shows, one by one, how important each crew member could be to the success of the mission, which is to please guests and crew members alike, starting with a smile and a greeting. There are many other tasks delegated to crew members daily, and skills are required of each. But the attitude of warmth toward crew and guest is the foundation for each job well done.

These conversations with crew members tell us something about the environment created by the organization's leaders. They imply that people at the top of an organization have a clear vision of how to organize and motivate people, notwithstanding the language and customs differences of people from many backgrounds and cultures. By seeking "how" the corporate culture can be spread and maintained, we might understand the recipe for the miracle of the "secret sauce" that Royal Caribbean International uses to encourage a blending of cultures and the creation of an unforgettable experience for the guests. There are people who spend much time interacting with guests and others whose main contacts are other crew members. The smile and the greeting symbolize the importance of every person aboard, and they open the door to further cooperation and friendship.

These stories reveal a crew culture that ensures "all hands work together" with cooperation and imagination, so guests have a happy and memorable cruise experience. On land or sea, the hospitality industry trains and motivates its people to please guests. This management team enjoys unusual success with cooperation among many different national cultures working on a single ship. Such a crew culture does not exist simply by accident or only because of good employee selection.

In dozens of stories, the answers to "how" vary with the individual, but the result is spectacular. New and veteran cruise guests can peek behind the scenes and learn about the ten-foot rule and many other secrets of the cruise industry. Supervisors and trainers can develop ways to encourage multi-cultural cooperation among their diverse employees. All types of entities, public, private and not for profit can learn from the ideas expressed by people who bear a striking resemblance to ourselves.

The author's interviewees reveal the secrets of how to motivate and train such employees. The United Nations, and the cultures they represent, could be

another possible crucible for attempting to encourage respect for our differences. If our own organizations fostered the type of cultural admiration expressed on these pages, and our planet's nations applied the 10-foot-rule during
all worldwide encounters, imagine the contagion that would foster! Perhaps
this can be more than a business book if many readers took the stories to heart.
It's amazing how a simple thing like employer standards for people earning a
living could change the world's attitudes toward diversity. As one crewmember
put it, "Somehow, if you are black, if you are white, if I am small, if you are
tall, we have come here to work and earn money, and at the end of the day, we
are all winners if we work together."

**SEE COMMENTS AT END OF BOOK AND SUGGESTIONS FOR FURTHER READING.
OTHER AUTHORS HAVE INTERESTING IDEAS.**

[See also author page and other books by Jackie Chase.]

🦅 *Further Reading*

Related resources for top/middle/hopeful managers help create respect for the business mission and all stakeholders and are listed below.

'24/7' relates personal interview stories that provide examples to every reader showing how important they are to the mission of cultivating a firm's inside and outside relationships. It contains universal ideas they can adapt to any situations including those that involve people from unfamiliar backgrounds and cultures. The eBook is provided without charge by employers.

The following book titles can be ordered individually or in quantity and are primarily intended for managers of an organization, but those in the ranks who wish to add skills or climb the success ladder may also wish to peruse one or more of the titles. In some cases, as with BookShout, purchase links are provided. The books approach the topic of improving organizational culture, often analytically, in ways different from the informal stories for a general population in "24-7".

The www.InclusionPLUSdiversity.com and the www.AdventureTravelPress.com websites, will add new books, editorially sifted [selected] by relevant diversity criteria applied here. In "24-7", all organizations can access a variety of tools, warmly shared by words of crew members, to bridge cultural diversity, gender, age and other differences and accomplish great missions, all packaged in a "ready to email" format to be read by all employees.

In the following pages, a number of books are listed, in the spirit of "fair use" honoring those chosen with links to the supplier, expanding the toolkit into helpful areas for company managers, new, experienced, or hopeful.

Comments of any kind can be directed to the publisher by email at:

Publisher@InclusionPLUSdiversity.com

Useful links are set forth below:

The following URLs are footnotes to find relevant inclusion eBooks, courtesy of www.InclusionPLUSdiversity.com with thanks for privilege of fair use by distributor, BookShout.com :

https://www.bookshout.com/ebooks/**the-power-of-inclusion**

https://www.bookshout.com/ebooks/**building-on-the-promise-of-diversity**

https://www.bookshout.com/ebooks/**change-the-culture-change-the-game**

https://www.bookshout.com/ebooks/**cultivating-a-creative-culture**

https://www.bookshout.com/ebooks/**driven-by-difference**

https://www.bookshout.com/ebooks/**exclusion**

The following books [and many more eBooks and print books]

are available at www.bookshout.com.

https://www.bookshout.com/ebooks/hbr-s-**10-must-reads-on-managing-across-cultures**-with-featured-article-cultural-intelli-gence-by-p-christopher-earley-and-elaine-mosakowski

[**goo.gl/AvDmrA**   <<<Short URL for title above: *"10-must-reads..."*]

https://www.bookshout.com/ebooks/**leading-culture-change**

https://www.bookshout.com/ebooks/**overcoming-bias**

https://www.bookshout.com/ebooks/**permission-to-speak-freely**

https://www.bookshout.com/ebooks/**selling-women-short**--2

https://www.bookshout.com/ebooks/**the-diversity-bonus**

https://www.bookshout.com/ebooks/**the-millennial-myth**

https://www.bookshout.com/ebooks/**the-multicultural-mind**

https://www.bookshout.com/ebooks/**the-respectful-leader**--3

https://www.bookshout.com/ebooks/**the-xyz-factor**--2

https://www.bookshout.com/ebooks/**we-can-t-talk-about-that-at-work**

https://www.bookshout.com/ebooks/**why-should-anyone-work-here**

author page

Jackie Chase, [JackieChase.com, WorldTravelDiva.com, and CulturesOfThe-World.com], has traveled to over 100 countries and specializes in staying in remote villages in order to use her keen observations and photo-journalism skills to share her insights with her reader fans.

She has traveled alone, with a child, with family, and with friends; she has earned over 32 awards from international book contests from 2014 to date of printing; she shares with the public many of the travel secrets she has experienced in her book titled, *"How to Become an Escape Artist" A Traveler's Handbook.*

The Handbook was tested for several years with students in a college evening class, and they soaked up Jackie's hints and the many ways to avoid disappointment, reduce expenses and frustrations, navigate the issues of visas, language, customs, currencies, accommodations, transportation, attitudes, danger, travel alone, and other problems all covered in over 190 segments in the book. It is up to date with nearly 100 click links to hard-to-find websites dealing with all aspects of travel, including finding companions.

Her *"All Hands Working Together" Cruise for a Week: Meet 79 Cultures* book treats cruising in a unique way to learn about cultures; the reader experiences personal contact with crewmembers from many of the 79 countries they represent, and from many skills they possess.

Jackie Chase has written definitive books on "People to Meet" in contrast to "Places to See". She convinces her readership to look beyond mountains, lakes and buildings to see world inhabitants of all continents as potential friends and shows how much we have in common.

She shows how to bridge gaps created by custom and language in *"100 People to Meet before You Die: Travel to Exotic Places"*. This book, [as well as the others], are available in color, grayscale, and, with stunning images in eBooks that come to life on backlit screens. This anthology involves 12 countries and contains 321 of those story-telling images and ward-winning prose about her adventures. For her fans of a particular country, she has twelve "singles" in print and in eBook format, plus at least one (Panama) translated into Spanish.

For children, from small up through teens, a "winner" of a book is *"Giraffe-Neck Girl" Make Friends with Different Cultures*. It is about a ten-year-old girl in Thailand who warms the hearts of young and old as she shares her different life and customs.

Jackie Chase's 2016 book, *"Walking to Woot" A Photographic Narrative Discovering New Dimensions for Parent-Teen Bonding* has won 17 international awards in the genres of Parenting, Young Adult Non-fiction, Multi-Cultural, Cover Design and Travel, and it contains both poetic descriptions and visual ones with its nearly 170 images of life with stone-age tribal warriors who haven't changed customs in a thousand years. The New Guinea unclothed villagers welcomed Jackie and her blond 14-year-old daughter to pig roasts, unusual customs, and dances. Jackie Chase loves to hear from her fans and to see copies of reviews they submit to the web. Contact her at:

JakartaMoon@hotmail.com

BOOKS BY JACKIE CHASE: 2014/16
How to Become an Escape Artist: A Traveler's Handbook (2014-6)
Giraffe-Neck Girl: Make Friends with a Different Culture (2014)
100 People to Meet before You Die: Travel to Exotic Cultures (2014-6)

AWARDS (15) FOR THE BOOKS LISTED ABOVE
Royal Palm Literary Award; National Indie Excellence Book Award; FAPA President's Book Award; Readers' Favorite Book Award; International Book Award; USA Best Book Award; Beverly Hills Book Awards

AWARDS (17) For: "Walking to Woot" A Photographic Narrative Discovering New Dimensions for Parent-Teen Bonding: Beach Book: & San Francisco: Festivals; Beverly Hills Book Award in 3 Genres; Eric Hoffer Grand Prize Award in 2 Genres; Florida Authors and Publishers Association (FAPA, including cover award); International Book Award, Montaigne Medals; National Indie Excellence Award; Next Generation Indie Book Award in 2 Genres; Paris Book: Festival; Reader's Favorite Award in 3 Genres.

BUSINESS BOOK BY JACKIE CHASE: 2017
'24-7' Multi-Cultural Workers Find Diversity Recipe to Heal a Troubled World [Sharing inclusion/diversity ideas with employees/students/managers in businesses, charities and governments using inexpensive eBook distribution methods to reach every participant in the organization].

All books available: www.AdventureTravelPress.com and www.inclusion-PLUSdiversity.com

'24-7' Multi-Cultural Workers Find Diversity Recipe to Heal a Troubled World

You have peeked behind the scenes of the world's largest floating resort to see how 79 different cultures work and live together '24-7'. Universally relevant stories created an inclusion recipe that celebrates human differences including race, customs, gender, age, religion etc. They open minds to cross-cultural awareness or respect in organizations worldwide. Current technology makes it possible to deliver an eBook to every worker in an organization to enhance its mission and stimulate a widely-shared attitude adjustment that produces success through cooperative creativity. Diversity at work pays creativity dividends for employer and worker. Imagine applying this team-building magic in government, campus, non-profit or business settings!

Jackie Chase
No stranger to travel, this photo-journalist has lived among many cultures to observe daily life in 100+ countries. Garnering over 32 competition awards for her 5 major books, she observes and shares stories about the lives of remote villagers and fascinating cultures. Here, the "villagers" share a ship while discovering secrets to harmonious ways cultures can live and work together. Please help her spread these stories of respect and inclusion by sharing this book with your friends and family.

E-book: ISBN-978-1-937630-31-7

www.ingramcontent.com/pod-product-compliance
Lightning Source LLC
Chambersburg PA
CBHW061315220326

41599CB00026B/4893